McGraw-Hill's
CHINESE
PRONUNCIATION

McGraw-Hill's
CHINESE
PRONUNCIATION

Your comprehensive, interactive guide
to mastering sounds and tones in Chinese

New York Chicago San Francisco Lisbon London Madrid Mexico City
Milan New Delhi San Juan Seoul Singapore Sydney Toronto

1 2 3 4 5 6 7 8 9 10 11 12 13 14 15 16 17 18 19 20   CTP/CTP   0 9

ISBN 978-0-07-162736-8 (book and CD set)
MHID   0-07-162736-7 (book and CD set)

ISBN 978-0-07-162734-4 (book for set)
MHID   0-07-162734-0 (book for set)

Library of Congress Control Number: 2008939330

McGraw-Hill books are available at special quantity discounts to use as premiums and sales promotions, or for use in corporate training programs. To contact a representative please e-mail us at bulksales@mcgraw-hill.com.

MP3 Disk

The accompanying disk contains MP3 recordings of all terms presented in this book. These files can be played on all MP3 players.

For optimum use on the iPod:

1. Open iTunes on your computer.
2. Insert the disk into your computer and open via My Computer.
3. Drag the folder "Copy to iTunes Music Library" into Music in the iTunes menu. For older/slower computers, it is suggested that you first open this folder and drag the three folders within to iTunes separately.
4. Sync your iPod with iTunes and eject the iPod.
5. Locate the recordings on your iPod by following this path:
    Main menu: **Menu**
    Music menu: **Artists**
    Artist menu: **Chinese Pronunciation: Topics (follows track order)**
             (for page-by-page ordering of all entries)

CONTENTS

CONTENTS

UNIT 2
UNIT 3
REVIEW 1
UNIT 5
REVIEW 2
UNIT 9
REVIEW 3
UNIT 10
UNIT 11
UNIT 12
REVIEW 4
UNIT 15
UNIT 16
UNIT 17
REVIEW 5
UNIT 18
UNIT 19
UNIT 20
UNIT 21
REVIEW 6
UNIT 22
UNIT 23
UNIT 24
REVIEW 7
APPENDIX
ANSWER KEY

PREFACE

Dr. Liang-Kuang Chen of Taiwan's Kaohsiung Normal University, Ms. I-Chen Hsu of the World Chinese Language Education Association, and Hebron Soft Limited have worked together to focus on the needs of learners from English-speaking countries who study Mandarin Chinese. This book is the result of that effort. When Hebron Soft Limited commissioned me to write a preface for the book, I carefully read and reread it. Looking at the pronunciation theory of the book, I could see that the system is complete and the phonetic sounds are accurate. The book completely describes initial sounds, vowel sounds, and tones, and any teachers or learners that use it will gain a comprehensive understanding of Chinese pronunciation.

The book uses diagrams as well as text to describe Chinese phonetic pronunciation and clearly shows the four tones of Chinese. The illustration descriptions are eloquent, intuitive, and brief. They enable the learner to quickly understand and imitate the way the sounds are created. In order to increase the effectiveness of the learning process, this book uses audio, visual, and text together for a three-dimensional learning process.

When learners from an English-speaking country study Chinese, due to the influence of their native tongue, their pronunciation is often wrong or imprecise. This book counteracts this problem by attempting to perfect the ear of a learner first so that subsequent pronunciation lessons are more effective. In addition, the authors aim to make learning fun and put the newly learned sounds into songs and chants. In these songs and chants, the learner can better feel and enjoy the sounds, which helps aid in their absorption.

The editor of this book uses the compare-and-contrast method to highlight and explain difficult sounds and tones. The book takes pains to help learners overcome common pronunciation difficulties. I believe that learners using this book will certainly learn in a much more efficient manner. In short, this pronunciation guide is based on scientific principles and is systematic, simple, targeted, and practical. I think that this book will prove an invaluable aid for learners who truly want to learn Chinese.

Ocean University of China
College of Language, Journalism and Communications

LETTER FROM THE EDITOR

In recent years, as Chinese has become popular all over the world, a huge number of Chinese learning materials covering different learning methods have been published. Chinese is different than Romanized languages in that, if you want to speak it well, you must start with pronunciation and the pinyin system. Many beginners want to immediately start speaking and communicating with others in Chinese, but if the learner doesn't first start with pronunciation and pinyin, it will lead to a lot of embarrassment and misunderstandings.

Chinese Pronunciation uses Chinese pinyin as a foundation. Divided into 24 lesson units, the book is designed to make use of spiral learning by inserting review material when new material is introduced. This helps the learner gain a firmer grasp of the material and progress faster. Each unit introduces initial or final sounds and uses examples from daily life to help the learner integrate the initial, final, and tone in a natural fashion. Each unit is also packed with colloquialisms and phrases that can be used in everyday life.

Every unit begins with a phonetic unit and includes six parts:
Part One: Simple Pinyin Sounds
Part Two: Combining Sounds
Part Three: Read Out Loud
Part Four: Speak and Sing
Part Five: Practical Sentences
Part Six: Give It a Try

Every few units, there is a "review unit." These units pose interesting questions to increase practice opportunities and help the learner become more familiar with pronunciation, pinyin, and tones.

Learning Chinese includes the four skills of listening, speaking, reading, and writing. Due to needs of modern language and the importance of the Internet, many scholars believe that pinyin, translation, and typing should also be included among these skills. However, pronunciation is still the most fundamental part of Chinese language study. This book is different than other Chinese pronunciation books on the market in that it combines sound pronunciation principles with effective pronunciation practice in such a way that it may be quickly used in day-to-day life. By using these learning materials, learners will be able to quickly grasp the fundamentals of pronunciation, pinyin, and tones and be on the way to fluent, standard Chinese.

HOW TO USE THIS BOOK

When using this book, follow the instructions and learning principles contained therein in order to obtain the best possible results.

 1

This unit focuses on specific pinyin combinations, showing learners how to combine pinyin using the four Chinese tones.

Unit Name

Unit Introducing Pinyin Combinations

Unit Introducing Important Points about Pinyin

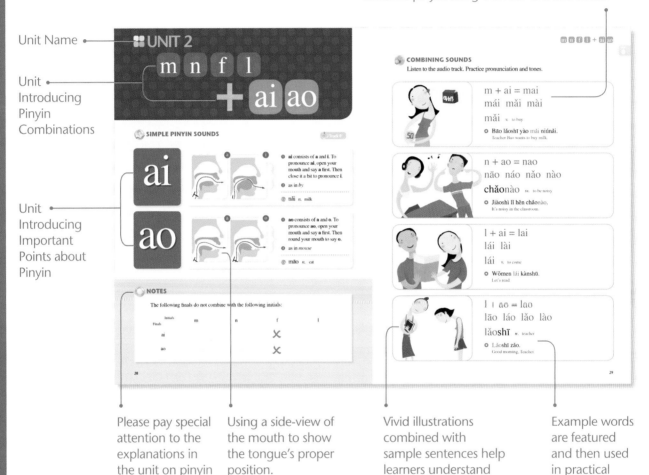

Please pay special attention to the explanations in the unit on pinyin combinations.

Using a side-view of the mouth to show the tongue's proper position.

Vivid illustrations combined with sample sentences help learners understand and remember new phrases.

Example words are featured and then used in practical sentence patterns.

Please note the following:

❶ Pinyin is spelled according to the "Basic Rules for Hanyu Pinyin Orthography" and "Xīnhuá Pīnxiě Cídiǎn."

❷ Terms that specifically relate to Chinese are also used. Abbreviations for these terms are listed in the table on the right:

adv.	Adverb	*pron.*	Pronoun
m.	Measure Word	*sv.*	Stative Verb
n.	Noun	*t.*	Time Word
nu.	Number	*v.*	Verb
prep.	Preposition		

2

Using chants and songs, learners can practice pronunciation in a relaxing manner. Differently colored characters remind learners to pay close attention to phonetic combinations.

At the end of each unit, a review test allows learners to review and assess their progress.

Each unit can be used with the CD-ROM / MP3.

Confusing pinyin combinations have been taken from the unit to give the learner pronunciation comparison practice.

The pinyin combinations in this unit help develop practical language skills for day-to-day life.

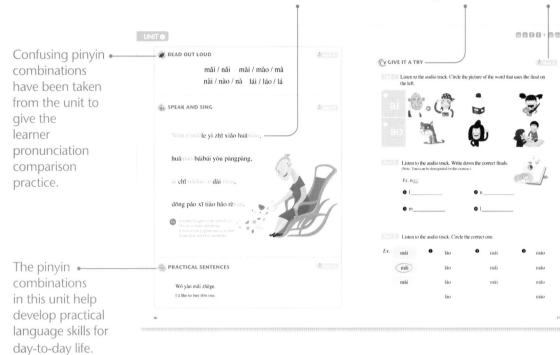

3

Every few units, there is a review chapter. These chapters use a variety of methods to review the materials and integrate what the learner has already learned.

HOW TO USE THE CD-ROM

System Requirements:

- PC Pentium II compatible or above

- Operating system: MS-Window 98 or above

- 256 MB RAM

- CD-ROM drive: 8X speed or above

- High-color display: 16-bit color or above

- Sound card, speaker, and microphone

- Microsoft Media Player 9

Main Menu

Click on Unit in the Main Menu to learn pinyin. Click on the pinyin symbols to see a video demonstration.

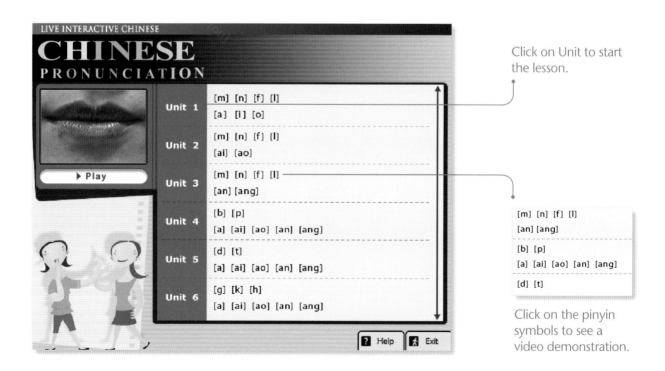

Click on Unit to start the lesson.

Click on the pinyin symbols to see a video demonstration.

Each unit has six learning components. These include *Simple Pinyin Sounds*, *Combining Sounds*, *Read Out Loud*, *Speak and Sing*, *Practical Sentences*, and *Give It a Try*. All six components are designed to help learners better understand pinyin.

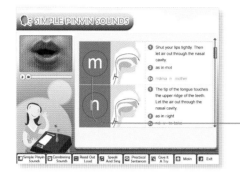

Simple Pinyin Sounds

The demonstration videos and pronunciation position pictures help learners pronounce the sounds correctly.

  Click on the pinyin symbol to see the video demonstration.

Combining Sounds

A video demonstration helps learners to combine sounds and change tones.

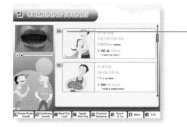

  Click on the film symbol to see the video demonstration.

Speak and Sing

Singing, Lyrics, and Karaoke provide three options for learners to practice pinyin.

The color of the lyrics changes with the melody.

Practice pinyin using the Singing, Lyrics, and Karaoke functions.

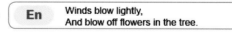

Learners are also provided with English translations.

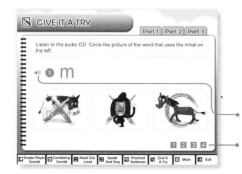

Give It a Try

Each unit has a review section to help learners evaluate their progress.

  Click on the microphone icon to listen to the question. Then, choose the correct answer.

 Go to the next question.

1. The basic structure of the Chinese syllables

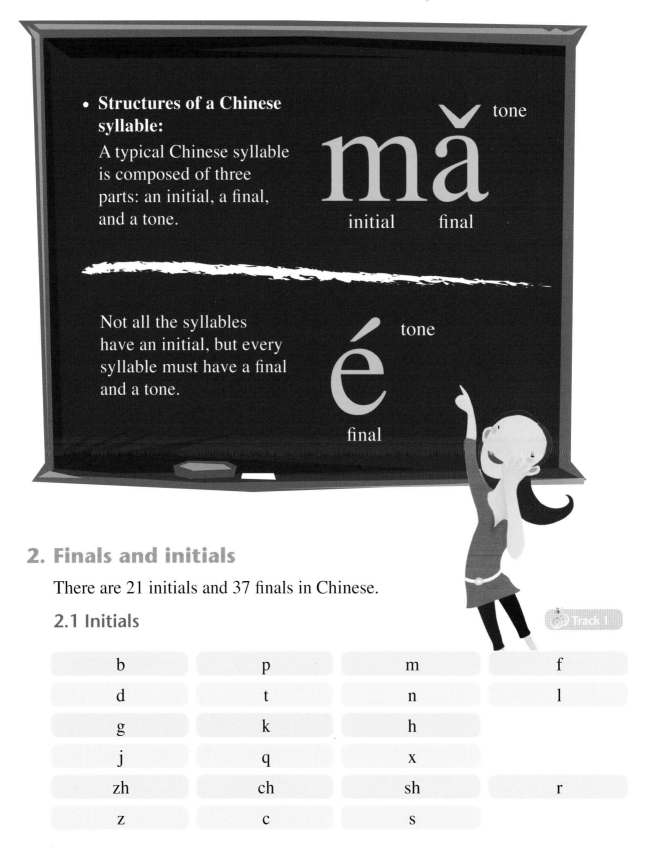

- **Structures of a Chinese syllable:**

  A typical Chinese syllable is composed of three parts: an initial, a final, and a tone.

  mǎ

  tone · initial · final

  Not all the syllables have an initial, but every syllable must have a final and a tone.

  é

  tone · final

2. Finals and initials

There are 21 initials and 37 finals in Chinese.

2.1 Initials

Track 1

b	p	m	f
d	t	n	l
g	k	h	
j	q	x	
zh	ch	sh	r
z	c	s	

a	o	e	ê	
i	u	ü		
ai	ei	ao	ou	
an	en	ang	eng	ong
er				
ia	ie	iao	iu [1]	
ian	in	iang	ing	iong
ua	uo	uai	ui [2]	
uan	un [3]	uang	ueng	
üe	üan	ün		

For the sake of economy, some vowels are omitted in pinyin orthography. For example, **iu**[1] is pronounced **iou**, but the **o** is omitted and it is written as **iu**. Also, **ui**[2] and **un**[3] are pronounced **uei** and **uen**, but the **e** is omitted and they are written as **ui** and **un**.

When there is no initial consonant before **i**, **u**, **ü**:

i	i is written as y, or y is added before the syllable	i → yi, ia → ya, ie → ye, iao → yao, iu → you, ian → yan, iang → yang, in → yin, ing → ying, iong → yong
u	u is written as w, or w is added before the syllable	u → wu, ua → wa, uo → wo, uai → wai, ui → wei, uan → wan, un → wen, uang → wang, ueng → weng
ü	y is added before the syllable (the two dots can be dropped)	ü → yu, üan → yuan, üe → yue, ün → yun

3. Tones

 Track 3

Tones are the pitch of a syllable. They are an important element of the Chinese syllable. The main function of the tones is to distinguish the meanings of the characters. For example, **shuǐjiǎo** (dumplings) and **shuìjiào** (to sleep). Their initials and finals are the same, but with different tones, the meanings are different. Chinese has four basic tones and a neutral tone:

basic tones				neutral tone
1st	2nd	3rd	4th	
mā	má	mǎ	mà	māma
n. mother	*n.* hemp	*n.* horse	*v.* to scold	*n.* mother

3.1 The tonal value of four basic tones

The pitches of the four tones are illustrated in the diagram below.

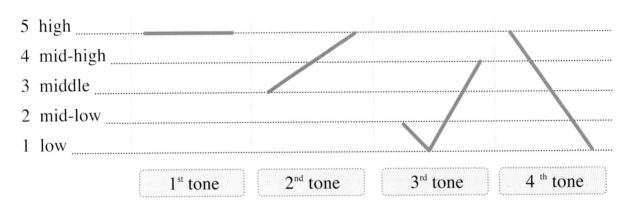

5 high
4 mid-high
3 middle
2 mid-low
1 low

| 1st tone | 2nd tone | 3rd tone | 4th tone |

- The 1st tone is a high, level tone. It is a steady, high pitch and is the highest of the four tones. Remember to maintain the high level pitch from the beginning to the end of the syllable.

- The 2nd tone is a high, rising tone. It begins at about the middle of the voice range and rises rapidly to the top. Remember to raise your tone voice as if you're asking a question.

- The 3rd tone is a low, dipping tone. It starts quite low, then goes even lower, and quickly rises up. It is maintained a little longer than the other tones. Remember to start your tone at a low enough level.

- The 4th tone starts high and goes down sharply and quickly. This tone is held less time than any of the others. Remember to make your voice go down as quickly as possible.

3.2 The neutral tone

The neutral tone is toneless. It is pronounced soft and short. In transcription, the neutral tone does not carry a tone mark. For example:

gēge	háizi	nǎinai	bàba
n. elder brother	*n.* child	*n.* grandmother	*n.* father

3.3 How to write tones

3.3.1 Tone marks are written above the main vowel of a syllable. The main vowel is determined by this order of precedence: **a – o – e – i – u – ü**. For example, in **ao**, the main vowel is **a**, and in **ei**, the main vowel is **e**. However, there is an exception with **i** and **u**. That is, when **i** and **u** exist in the same syllable, the tone mark is always placed on the second vowel. For example, **niú** (cow) and **duì** (correct).

3.3.2 The dot in the letter – **i** is removed when a tone mark is placed over it. For example, **nǐ** (you) and **yī** (one).

3.3.3 The two dots of group – **ü** finals changes depending on the following situations:

–ü, -üē, -üān, -ün		
Remove the two dots		Keep the two dots
Stand alone	Combine with **j, q,** and **x**	Combine with **n** and **l**
Ex. **yuè, yuán**	Ex. **jú, qún**	Ex. **nǚ, lǜ**

Here are some more rules for the pinyin system.

1. Capital letters

❶ Capitalize the first letter of all proper nouns. For example, **Kǒngzǐ** (Confucius), **Xiānggǎng** (Hong Kong), and **Lǐ xiānsheng** (Mr. Lee).

❷ Capitalize the first letter of the first word in a sentence. For example, **"Píngguǒ yì jīn duōshǎo qián?"** (How much for one kilogram of apples?)

2. Pinyin basically follows the punctuation rules of English. The only difference is that, in Chinese, we use " 、 " to separate the items. For example, **"Wǒ xǐhuan píngguǒ、xiāngjiāo hé mùguā."** (I like apples, bananas, and papayas.)

3. In order to avoid confusion, an apostrophe (') is used to divide two syllables when the combination may cause uncertainty or ambiguity. For example, **jī'è** (hunger) and **píng'ān** (safety).

First, we will learn how to pronounce the following initials:

m n f l

Then, we will learn how to combine the initials with the following finals:

UNIT 1 a i o P. 22

UNIT 1

m n f l + a i o

 SIMPLE PINYIN SOUNDS

❶ Shut your lips tightly. Then let air out through the nasal cavity.

❷ as in *mat*

Ex māma *n.* mother

❶ The tip of the tongue touches the upper ridge of the teeth. Let the air out through the nasal cavity.

❷ as in *night*

Ex ná *v.* to take

 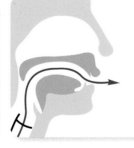

❶ Press the upper teeth against the lower lip. Let out a breath. The sound relies on friction between the teeth and the lip.

❷ as in *fat*

Ex fà *n.* hair

 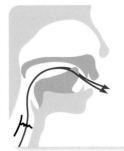

❶ The tip of the tongue touches the back of the upper ridge of the teeth. Let the air out from both sides of the tongue.

❷ as in *light*

Ex lā *v.* to pull

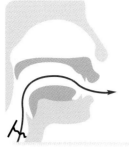

❶ Open your mouth wide and keep your tongue in a flat, relaxed position.

❷ as in *father*

Ex bàba *n.* father

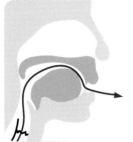

❶ Keep your mouth flat as if you were pronouncing the English letter E.

❷ as in *eat*

Ex yī *nu.* one

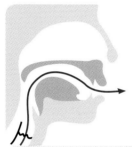

❶ Make your mouth round and hold your tongue in the middle.

❷ There is no identical sound in English.

Ex mō *v.* to touch

NOTES

❶ The following finals do not combine with the following initials:

Finals \ Initials	m	n	f	l
a				
i			X	
o		X		X

❷ If there is no initial before **i**, it is spelled **yi**.

COMBINING SOUNDS

Listen to the audio track. Practice pronunciation and tones.

m + a = ma

mā má mǎ mà

māma *n.* mother

○ Wǒ ài māma.
I love my mom.

n + a = na

nā ná nǎ nà

ná *v.* to take

○ Wǒ ná xīguā.
I hold a watermelon.

f + a = fa

fā fá fǎ fà

tóufa *n.* hair

○ Mǎ xiǎojiě bāng wǒ jiǎn tóufa.
Miss Ma helps me to cut my hair.

l + a = la

lā lá lǎ là

lā *v.* to pull

○ Tā wàngle lā chuānglián.
He forgot to pull the window curtains closed.

 NOTES

When we refer to "hair," there are two different pronunciation ways in Chinese. When we say **fà**, it is 4th tone; however, when we say **tóufa**, it becomes neutral tone.

m + i = mi

mī mí mǐ mì

bǎomì *v.* to keep the secret

○ Qǐng nǐ yídìng yào bǎomì.
Please be sure to keep the secret.

n + i = ni

nī ní nǐ nì

nǐ *pron.* you

○ Nǐ shì Měiguó rén ma?
Are you American?

l + i = li

lī lí lǐ lì

lìqi *n.* (physical) strength, force

○ Bàba de lìqi hěn dà.
My father is very powerful.

m + o = mo

mō mó mǒ mò

mō *v.* to touch

○ Zhè jiàn yīfu mō qǐlái hěn shūfu.
This shirt feels very comfortable.

 READ OUT LOUD

mǎ / nǎ   fā / lā   má / ná   fà / là

mí / ní / lí   má / mó   mó / fó

 Track 6

SPEAK AND SING

yī   èr   sān sì   wǔ   liù   qī   wǒ de lǐwù zài   nǎlǐ

zài nǎlǐ   zài nǎlǐ   wǒ de lǐwù zài   nǎlǐ   qī liù wǔ sì sān   èr   yī

wǒ de lǐwù zài   zhèlǐ   zài zhèlǐ   zài zhèlǐ   wǒ de lǐwù zài   zhèlǐ

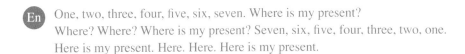

lǐwù   xiǎomǎ (little horse)   /   māomī (kitty)   /   jiǎfà (wig)

En One, two, three, four, five, six, seven. Where is my present?
Where? Where? Where is my present? Seven, six, five, four, three, two, one.
Here is my present. Here. Here. Here is my present.

 PRACTICAL SENTENCES

Nǐ hǎo!   Hi!

Nǐ hǎo ma?   How are you?

GIVE IT A TRY

Part 1 Listen to the audio track. Circle the picture of the word that uses the initial on the left.

Part 2 Listen to the audio track. Choose the correct finals.

	a	i	o
Ex.	✓		
1			
2			
3			
4			

Part 3 Listen to the audio track. Circle the correct word.

Ex.	❶	❷	❸
(má)	nǐ	fá	nà
mǎ	lǐ	fó	là

UNIT 2

m n f l + ai ao

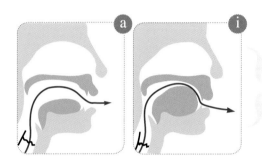

❶ **ai** consists of **a** and **i**. To pronounce **ai**, open your mouth and say **a** first. Then close it a bit to pronounce **i**.

❷ as in *by*

Ex **nǎi** *n.* milk

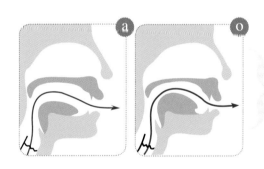

❶ **ao** consists of **a** and **o**. To pronounce **ao**, open your mouth and say **a** first. Then round your mouth to say **o**.

❷ as in *mouse*

Ex **māo** *n.* cat

 NOTES

The following finals do not combine with the following initials:

Initials Finals	m	n	f	l
ai			✗	
ao			✗	

28

COMBINING SOUNDS

Listen to the audio track. Practice pronunciation and tones.

m + ai = mai

mái mǎi mài

mǎi *v.* to buy

○ Bāo lǎoshī yào mǎi niúnǎi.
Teacher Bao wants to buy milk.

n + ao = nao

nāo náo nǎo nào

chǎonào *sv.* to be noisy

○ Jiàoshì lǐ hěn chǎonào.
It's noisy in the classroom.

l + ai = lai

lái lài

lái *v.* to come

○ Wǒmen lái kànshū.
Let's read.

l + ao = lao

lāo láo lǎo lào

lǎoshī *n.* teacher

○ Lǎoshī zǎo.
Good morning, Teacher.

READ OUT LOUD

măi / năi   mài / mào / mà

nài / nào / nà   lái / láo / lá

SPEAK AND SING

Năinai măile yì zhī xiǎo huāmāo,

huāmāo báibái yòu pàngpàng,

ài chī năilào ài dài mào,

dōng pǎo xī tiào hǎo rènao.

En Grandma bought a little spotted cat.
The cat is white and plump.
It loves to eat yoghurt and wear a hat.
It runs here and there mirthfully.

PRACTICAL SENTENCES

Wǒ yào mǎi zhège.

I'd like to buy this one.

GIVE IT A TRY

Part 1 Listen to the audio track. Circle the picture of the word that uses the final on the left.

Part 2 Listen to the audio track. Write down the correct finals.
(Note: Tones can be disregarded for this exercise.)

Ex. n<u>ao</u>

❶ l_____   ❷ n_____

❸ m_____   ❹ l_____

Part 3 Listen to the audio track. Circle the correct one.

Ex.	❶	❷	❸
mái	lāo	mái	māo
(măi)	láo	măi	máo
mài	lǎo	mài	mǎo
	lào		mào

UNIT 3

m n f l

+ an ang

📖 **SIMPLE PINYIN SOUNDS**

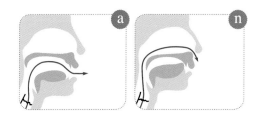

① Open your mouth and say **a** first. Then close it a bit to let the air out through the nasal cavity ending with **n**.

② as in *can (but open mouth more widely)*

Ex nán *n.* male

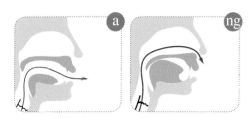

① Open your mouth and say **a** first. Then let the air out through the back part of the nasal cavity ending with **ng**.

② as in *among (but open mouth more widely)*

Ex máng *sv.* to be busy

COMBINING SOUNDS

Listen to the audio track. Practice pronunciation and tones.

m + an = man

mān mán mǎn màn

màn**pǎo** *v.* to jog

○ Wǒ měitiān zǎoshàng màn**pǎo**.
I jog every morning.

f + ang = fang

fāng fáng fǎng fàng

fáng**zi** *n.* house

○ Zhège fáng**zi** hěn piàoliang.
This house is very beautiful.

n + an = nan

nān nán nǎn nàn

nán**shēng** *n.* boy

○ Wǒmen bān yǒu sān ge nán**shēng**.
There are three boys in our class.

l + ang = lang

lāng láng lǎng làng

kāi**lǎng** *sv.* to be open-minded

○ Tā shì yí ge kāi**lǎng** de nǚhái.
She is an open-minded girl.

READ OUT LOUD

Track 15

mǎn / mǎng   nán / náng   fān / fāng   làn / làng

má / mán / máng   fà / fàn / fàng

SPEAK AND SING

Track 16

Yì tiān dúwán liǎng běn shū, lǎn lǎn lǎn.

Sān tiān xiěwán sìshí kè, màn màn màn.

Wǔ tiān shuōwán liùbǎi jù, máng máng máng.

Qī tiān tīngwán bāqiān cí, fán fán fán.

Jiǔ tiān dǎwán shíwàn zì, nán nán nán.

En   Reading two books in one day. Lazy, lazy, lazy.
Writing forty lessons in three days. Slow, slow, slow.
Saying six hundred sentences in five days. Busy, busy, busy.
Listening to eight thousand terms in seven days.
Annoying, annoying, annoying.
Typing one hundred thousand words in nine days.
Difficult, difficult, difficult.

PRACTICAL SENTENCES

Track 17

Qǐng shuō màn yìdiǎnr.

Please speak a little bit slowly.

Part 1 Listen to the audio track. Circle the picture of the word that uses the final on the left.

Part 2 Listen to the audio track. Write down the correct finals.
(Note: Tones can be disregarded for this exercise.)

Ex. f __an__

❶ n_____ ❷ l_____

❸ f_____ ❹ l_____

Part 3 Listen to the audio track. Circle the correct one.

Ex.	❶	❷	❸
fān	lán	fāng	nāng
(fán)	lǎn	fáng	náng
fǎn	làn	fǎng	nǎng
fàn		fàng	nàng

Part 1 Listen to the audio track. Circle the correct sound.

Ex.

(mama)

mǎmà

mámá

1.

máo

náo

lǎo

2.

ná

nǎi

nǎo

3.

mī

mí

mǐ

4.

fáng

fǎng

fàng

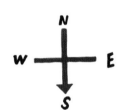

5.

nán

nǎn

nàn

Part 2 Listen to the phonetic finals of each pair of words on the audio track. If their finals have the same pronunciation, circle Yes. Otherwise, circle No.

Ex. Yes (No)

1. Yes No   **2.** Yes No

3. Yes No   **4.** Yes No

5. Yes No   **6.** Yes No

Part 3 Listen to the audio track. Match the initials and finals.
(Note: Tones can be disregarded for this exercise.)

Ex.

m   ang

1.

n   ai

2.

f   an

3.

l   a

Part 4 Listen to the audio track. Fill in the missing initials and finals.

1.	3.		2.		
				4.	
				à	
			g	ă	
	á				

In the previous units, we have learned the finals below:

a   ai   ao   an

Now, we will learn how to combine the finals with the following initials:

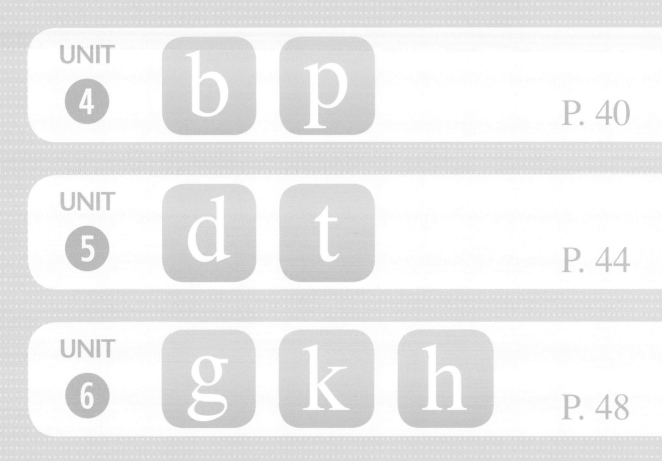

ang

UNIT 4

b p

SIMPLE PINYIN SOUNDS

1. Shut the lips tightly to obstruct breathing. Then open them to let out the air. This sound is not aspirated.

2. as in *bay*

Ex **bǎo** *sv.* to be full

 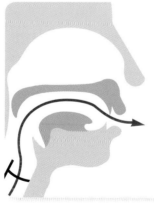

1. Like with **b**, the lips are shut tightly to obstruct breathing. Open them quickly and force the air out. This sound is aspirated.

2. as in *pop*

Ex **pàng** *sv.* to be fat

 COMBINING SOUNDS

Listen to the audio track. Practice pronunciation and tones.

b + ao = bao

bāo báo bǎo bào

bāozi *n.* steamed bun

○ Bàba chī bāozi.
Dad eats steamed buns.

p + a = pa

pā pá pà

pà *v.* to be afraid

○ Wǒ dìdi hěn pà gǒu.
My younger brother is very afraid of dogs.

b + ang = bang

bāng bǎng bàng

bāng *v.* to help, to assist

○ Wǒ bāng nǎinai ná dōngxi.
I helped my grandmother to pick up some stuff.

p + ao = pao

pāo páo pǎo pào

sàipǎo *v.* to have a race

○ Wǒmen lái sàipǎo ba!
Let's have a race!

 READ OUT LOUD

bà / pà   bái / pái   bǎo / pǎo   bān / pān   bàng / pàng
pā / pāi / pāo   bǎ / bǎn / bǎng

 SPEAK AND SING

Pàng xiǎodì, chī ròubāo,

chuān xīnpáo, fàng biānpào,

tiào yí tiào, diē yì jiāo,

pāipai pìgu jìxù pǎo.

En The chubby boy ate a meat bun,
Put on a new robe, set off fireworks,
Jumped around, and then fell down.
He dusted off his backside and ran off.

 PRACTICAL SENTENCES

Nǐ néng bāng wǒ ma?

Could you give me a hand?

📝 **GIVE IT A TRY**   🎧 **Track 24**

Part 1   Listen to the audio track. Circle the picture of the word that uses the initial on the left.

Part 2   Listen to the audio track. Choose the correct initials.

	b	p
Ex.	✓	
❶		
❷		
❸		
❹		

Part 3   Listen to the audio track. Circle the correct one.

Ex.	❶	❷	❸
bān	pāo	bāo	pā
(bǎn)	páo	báo	pá
bàn	pǎo	bǎo	pà
	pào	bào	

UNIT 5

d t + a ai ao an ang

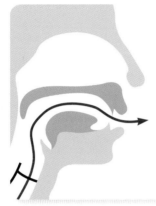

1. The tip of the tongue touches the upper ridge of the teeth. Drop the tongue to let out the air. The sound is not aspirated.

2. as in *dad*

Ex. dà *sv.* to be big

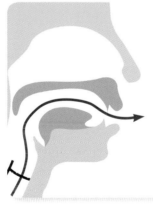

1. Like with **d**, the tip of the tongue touches the upper ridge of the teeth. Drop the tongue quickly to force the air out. This sound is aspirated.

2. as in *tap*

Ex. táng *n.* sugar

 COMBINING SOUNDS

Listen to the audio track. Practice pronunciation and tones.

d + a = da

dā dá dǎ dà

dǎ**qiú**   *v.*   to play ball

○ Wǒmen qù dǎqiú ba!
Let's play ball!

t + an = tan

tān tán tǎn tàn

tán**qín**   *v.*   to play the piano

○ Dài xiǎojiě huì tánqín ma?
Does Miss Dai know how to play the piano?

d + an = dan

dān dǎn dàn

dàn**gāo**   *n.*   cake

○ Dìdi ài chī cǎoméi dàngāo.
My younger brother likes to eat strawberry cake.

t + ang = tang

tāng táng tǎng tàng

tāng   *n.*   soup

○ Nǐ xǐhuan suānlàtāng ma?
Do you like hot and sour soup?

 READ OUT LOUD Track 26

dǎ / tǎ   dāi / tāi   dào / tào   dǎn / tǎn
dǎng / tǎng   da / dāi / dao   dà / dàn / dàng

 SPEAK AND SING Track 27

Xiàtiān dào, xiàtiān dào,

dàdà de tàiyáng dāngkōng zhào.

Tā táoqì, bú dài mào,

shāochéng hóngtàn gǎnkuài táopǎo.

En Summer is coming. Summer is coming.
The sun is shining brightly in the sky.
The boy is naughty. He doesn't wear a hat.
He is so sunburned that he has to run away.

 PRACTICAL SENTENCES Track 28

Nǐ duō dà le?

How old are you?

 **GIVE IT A TRY**

Part 1   Listen to the audio track. Circle the picture of the word that uses the initial on the left.

Part 2   Listen to the audio track. Write down the correct initials.

Ex. __t__ ā

❶ _____āo   ❷ _____án

❸ _____ào   ❹ _____àng

Part 3   Listen to the audio track. Circle the correct one.

Ex.	❶	❷	❸
tāo	dā	tān	tāng
táo	dá	tán	táng
tǎo	dǎ	tǎn	tǎng
tào	dà	tàn	tàng

g k h

+ a ai ao an ang

SIMPLE PINYIN SOUNDS

Track 30

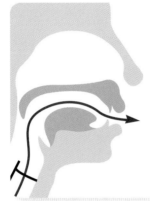

① Raise the back of your tongue against the soft palate. Then let out the air. This sound is not aspirated.

② as in *gold*

gāo *sv.* to be tall

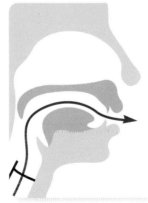

① Like with **g**, put the back of your tongue against the soft palate. Then let the air out, only this time with a bit more force. This sound is aspirated.

② as in *kangaroo*

kàn *v.* to look

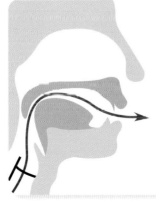

① Raise the back of your tongue toward the soft palate. Then let the air flow out the channel between the tongue and the soft palate.

② as in *house*

hǎi *n.* sea

COMBINING SOUNDS

Listen to the audio track. Practice pronunciation and tones.

g + an = gan

gān   gǎn   gàn

gānjìng   *sv.*   to be clean

○ Gēge de fángjiān hěn gānjìng.
My elder brother's room is very clean.

k + ang = kang

kāng   káng   kàng

jiànkāng   *sv.*   to be healthy

○ Zhù nǐ shēntǐ jiànkāng.
I wish you good health.

cinema

h + an = han

hān   hán   hǎn   hàn

hǎn   *v.*   to yell

○ Qǐng bú yào zài diànyǐngyuàn dà hǎn.
Please do not yell in the theater.

k + ao = kao

kāo   kǎo   kào

kǎoshì   *v.*   to take an exam
          n.   exam, test

○ Míngtiān wǒmen yào kǎoshì.
We will have an exam tomorrow.

49

READ OUT LOUD Track 31

gài / kài / hài   gǎo / kǎo / hǎo   gān / kān / hān
gàng / kàng / hàng   gà / gài / gào   há / hán / háng

 SPEAK AND SING Track 32

Gāo Dà'ān, lè kāihuái,

shēngrì dào, lǐwù lái,

hétao dàngāo yì dǎkāi,

Hā! Zhǐ shèng yìduī nǎiyóu lái!

En Gao Da-an was so happy.
His birthday was coming, and he received many presents.
He opened a present and it was a walnut cake.
Ha! There was nothing left but some cream!

 PRACTICAL SENTENCES Track 33

Zǎoshàng hǎo! / Xiàwǔ hǎo! / Wǎnshàng hǎo!

Good morning! / Good afternoon! / Good night!

GIVE IT A TRY

Part 1 Listen to the audio track. Circle the picture of the word that uses the initial on the left.

Part 2 Listen to the audio track. Choose the correct initials.

	g	k	h
Ex.	✓		
❶			
❷			
❸			
❹			

Part 3 Listen to the audio track. Circle the correct one.

Ex.
| kān |
| kǎn |
| (kàn) |

❶
| kāi |
| kǎi |
| kài |

❷
| hāo |
| háo |
| hǎo |
| hào |

❸
| gāng |
| gǎng |
| gàng |

Part 1 Listen to the audio track. Circle the correct sound. Track 35

Ex.

pāng

páng

(pàng)

1.

dān

dǎn

dàn

2.

gāo

gǎo

gào

3.

tāng

tǎng

tàng

4.

kān

kǎn

kàn

5.

bāozi

bózi

bàozi

Part 2 Listen to the phonetic initials of each pair of words on the audio track. If their initials have the same pronunciation, circle Yes. Otherwise, circle No.

Ex. (Yes)   No

1.   Yes   No

2.   Yes   No

3.   Yes   No

4.   Yes   No

5.   Yes   No

6.   Yes   No

Part 3

Listen to the audio track. Match the initials and finals.
(Note: Tones can be disregarded for this exercise.)

Ex.    b   ao

1.    t   a

2.   k   ai

3.   d   ang

Listen to the audio track. Fill in the missing initials and finals.

				4.	
		2.3. p		n	
1.	à				

UNIT 7

z zh

+ a ai ao an ang

 SIMPLE PINYIN SOUNDS Track 36

 **z**

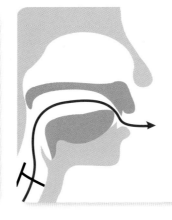

1. Place the tip of your tongue against the back of your teeth. Then let the air squeeze out between your tongue and teeth. This sound is not aspirated.
2. as in *birds*

Ex **zāng** *sv.* to be dirty

 **zh**

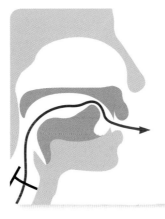

1. Turn up the tip of your tongue against the hard palate. Then loosen it a bit to let out the air. This sound is not aspirated.
2. as in *job*

Ex **zhǎi** *sv.* to be narrow

NOTES

z and **zh** are spelled **zi** and **zhi** when they stand alone.

COMBINING SOUNDS

Listen to the audio track. Practice pronunciation and tones.

z + a = za

zā zá zǎ

zázhì *n.* magazine

🔊 Wǒ ài kàn zázhì.
I love reading magazines.

zh + ao = zhao

zhāo zháo zhǎo zhào

zhǎo *v.* to look for

🔊 Gēge shàngwǎng zhǎo zīliào.
My elder brother surfed the Internet to find some information.

z + ao = zao

zāo záo zǎo zào

zǎofàn *n.* breakfast

🔊 Tā jīntiān méi chī zǎofàn.
He didn't have breakfast today.

zh + an = zhan

zhān zhǎn zhàn

zhàn *v.* to stand

🔊 Wǒ xǐhuan zhàn zài wǔtái shàng biǎoyǎn.
I like performing on stage.

Track 37

READ OUT LOUD

zǐ / zhǐ   zá / zhá   zài / zhài

zǎo / zhǎo   zān / zhān   zàng / zhàng

Track 38

SPEAK AND SING

Xiǎolǎoshǔ, zīzī jiào,

shàng le dēngtái, bǎozàng zhǎo.

Dōng zhǎozhao, xī zhǎozhao,

zhàn bù wěn jiù huádǎo.

Āiya! Zhēn zāogāo!

En   "Peep, peep, peep" says the mouse.
Go up the candlestick to look for treasure.
Look to the east. Look to the west.
Without a firm standing, the mouse slips and falls.
Ouch! It's terrible!

Track 39

PRACTICAL SENTENCES

Qing zài shuō yi ci.

Please say it again.

 **GIVE IT A TRY**

Part 1 Listen to the audio track. Circle the picture of the word that uses the initial on the left.

Part 2 Listen to the audio track. Write down the correct initials.

Ex. <u>zh</u> ān

❶ _____ài   ❷ _____ào

❸ _____ăng   ❹ _____á

Part 3 Listen to the audio track. Circle the correct one.

Ex.

(zhāi)
zhái
zhǎi
zhài

❶
zī
zǐ
zì

❷
zhān
zhǎn
zhàn

❸
zāo
záo
zǎo
zào

UNIT 8

c ch + a ai ao an ang

SIMPLE PINYIN SOUNDS

 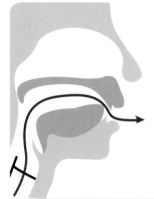

c

① Place the tip of your tongue against the back of your teeth. Then let a breath out, only stronger, through the channel between your tongue and teeth. This sound is aspirated.

② as in *cats (but with aspiration)*

Ex cài *n.* dish

 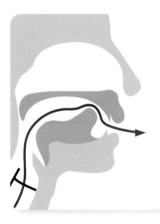

ch

① Turn up the tip of your tongue against the hard palate. Then loosen it a bit to let out the air, only with a stronger breath. This sound is aspirated.

② as in *chair*
(*but with the tongue tip curled far back and aspiration*)

Ex chā *n.* fork

NOTES

c and **ch** are spelled **ci** and **chi** when they stand alone.

COMBINING SOUNDS

Listen to the audio track. Practice pronunciation and tones.

c + a = ca

ca cǎ

cā *v.* to wipe

Wǒ bǎ jìngzi cā yi cā.
I wiped the mirror.

ch + a = cha

chā chá chǎ chà

chá *n.* tea

Cáo lǎoshī xǐhuan hē Zhōngguó chá.
Teacher Cao likes to drink Chinese tea.

c + an = can

cān cán cǎn càn

cāntīng *n.* restaurant

Cài xiǎojiě qù cāntīng chī wǎncān.
Miss Cai went to the restaurant to have dinner.

ch + ang = chang

chāng cháng chǎng chàng

lánqiúchǎng *n.* basketball court

Dàwèi zài lánqiúchǎng dǎqiú.
David played basketball on the basketball court.

READ OUT LOUD

 Track 42

cì / chì   cā / chā   cāi / chāi

căo / chăo   càn / chàn   cáng / cháng

SPEAK AND SING

 Track 43

Liăng piě xiăo húzi,

jiān zuĭ jiān yáchĭ,

cáng tóu yòu cáng năo,

xiăng zhăo dōngxi chī.

 En It has two little whiskers,
A sharp mouth and sharp teeth.
Hiding and moving like a thief,
It always wants to find food.

PRACTICAL SENTENCES

 Track 44

Yào duo cháng shíjiān?

How long will it take?

GIVE IT A TRY

Part 1 Listen to the audio track. Circle the picture of the word that uses the initial on the left.

Part 2 Listen to the audio track. Circle the correct word.

Ex.   (chī)   cī

❶   cāi   chāi   ❷   cáng   cháng

❸   cǎo   chǎo   ❹   càn   chàn

Part 3 Listen to the audio track. Circle the correct one.

Ex.

Ex.	❶	❷	❸
cān	cī	chāng	cha
cán	cí	cháng	chá
cǎn	cǐ	chǎng	chǎ
càn	cì	chàng	chà

UNIT 9

s sh r

+ a ai ao an ang

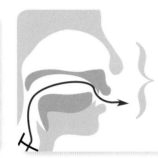

1. Place the tip of your tongue against the back of your teeth. Then let the air out between your tongue and teeth, as if you were pronouncing the **s** sound in English.

2. as in *sun*.

Ex. sān *nu.* three

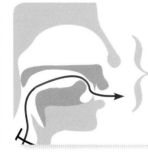

1. Turn up the tip of your tongue toward the hard palate. Then let the air squeeze out.

2. as in *share (but with the tongue tip curled further back)*

Ex. shǎo *sv.* few

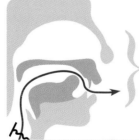

1. Turn up the tip of your tongue toward the hard palate to obstruct the breath. Then squeeze the air out.

2. as in *rain (but with the tongue tip curled further back)*

Ex. rǎn *v.* to dye

NOTES

1. The initial **r** does not combine with **a** and **ai**.

2. **s, sh,** and **r** are spelled **si, shi,** and **ri** when they stand alone.

COMBINING SOUNDS

Listen to the audio track. Practice pronunciation and tones.

s + an = san

sān sǎn sàn

sǎn *n.* umbrella

Xiàyǔtiān yào dài sǎn.
Take an umbrella on rainy days.

sh + an = shan

shān shǎn shàn

páshān *v.* to climb the mountain

Wǒ hé jiārén qù páshān.
I went mountain climbing with my family.

r + ang = rang

rāng ráng rǎng ràng

ràng**zuò** *v.* to offer one's seat to someone

Tā ràngzuò gěi yí wèi lǎorén.
He gave his seat to an old man.

s + ao = sao

sāo sǎo sào

dǎsǎo *v.* to clean

Jiālǐ dǎsǎo de hǎo gānjìng.
The house has been cleaned very well.

 Track 47

READ OUT LOUD

sì / shì   să / shă   sài / shài   săo / shăo   săn / shăn

sāng / shāng   răo / lăo   rán / lán   ràng / làng

 Track 48

SPEAK AND SING

Sì shì sì, shí shì shí, shísì shì shísì, sìshí shì sìshí.

Shísì bú shì shí shì, sìshí bú shì sì sī.

Xiăngyào shuō hăo sì hé shí,

měirì dōu yào duō liànxí.

En Sì (four) is sì, shí (ten) is shí,
shísì (fourteen) is shísì, sìshí (forty) is sìshí.
Shísì (fourteen) is not shí shì,
sìshí (forty) is not sì sī.
If you want to say sì (four) and shí (ten) well,
you need to practice more everyday.

 Track 49

PRACTICAL SENTENCES

Nĭ shì nă guó rén?

What's your nationality?

Track 50

e picture of the word that uses the initial

Part 2   Listen to the audio track. Write down the correct initials.

Ex. lǎo_sh_ī

❶ pá_____ān   ❷ _____ìjì   ❸ dǎ_____ǎo

Part 3   Listen to the audio track. Circle the correct one.

Ex.	❶	❷	❸
ráo	shī	shāo	sān
rǎo	shí	sháo	sǎn
(rào)	shǐ	shǎo	sàn
	shì	shào	

Part 1   Listen to the audio track. Circle the correct sound.

🔊 **Track 51**

Ex.

sān

(săn)

sàn

1.

zhāng

zháng

zhàng

2.

zāng

zǎng

zàng

3.

shān

shǎn

shàn

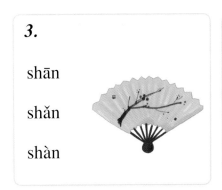

4.

chā

chá

chà

5.

cái

cǎi

cài

Part 2   Listen to the audio track. Fill in the missing initials and finals.

			3. **5.**	ān
			ǎ	
2. **4.**		á		
1.	ī			

Part 3 Listen the audio track. Choose the correct initials and finals from below.
(Note: Tones can be disregarded for this exercise.)

❶ zh ❷ sh ❸ z ❹ c ❺ r ❻ an ❼ a ❽ ao ❾ ang ❿ ai

Ex. [1 , 7]   1. [   ]   2. [   ]   3. [   ]   4. [   ]

Part 4 Circle all of the initials that require turning up the tongue to find the Chinese character hidden in the puzzle.

an	ai	ao	b	t	d	c	z	n	m	b	f	d
c	g	p	eng	q	l	d	q	eng	t	x	h	m
c	l	t	n	l	t	zh	x	t	an	d	a	l
f	j	b	ang	ai	en	zh	g	b	m	z	en	h
n	h	k	b	l	z	r	a	q	c	k	a	d
en	ch	x	m	c	x	zh	t	d	x	b	r	t
g	ch	ai	en	ang	h	zh	eng	x	p	f	zh	p
f	r	m	d	n	t	ch	z	n	k	j	zh	k
m	r	q	k	an	j	ch	m	g	an	z	ch	s
ang	r	ai	n	l	h	r	n	c	n	c	ch	c
ao	zh	k	c	m	a	r	s	b	q	s	sh	s
p	zh	b	g	h	t	sh	an	b	p	ang	sh	ang
ai	zh	x	l	s	h	ch	g	g	f	s	r	a
g	sh	r	r	ch	sh	ch	sh	zh	zh	r	r	d
n	g	z	d	m	h	b	t	l	z	f	s	g

Now, we will combine the initials with the finals below.

b p m f

g k h z

ch r

UNIT 10 o u ou P. 70

d t n l

c s zh sh

UNIT 10

b p m f d t n l g k h z

c s z zh ch sh r

+ o u ou

📖 **SIMPLE PINYIN SOUNDS** Track 52

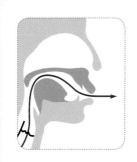

❶ Round your lips as if you were pronouncing "oo" in English.

❷ as in *blue*

....

Ex wǔ *nu.* five

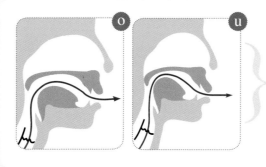

❶ **ou** consists of **o** and **u**. To pronounce **ou**, round your mouth and say **o** first. Then make your mouth even smaller to say **u**.

❷ as in *go*

....

Ex tóu *n.* head

💡 **NOTES**

❶ The following finals do not combine with the following initials:

Finals \ Initials	b	p	m	f	d	t	n	l	g	k	z	h	c	s	zh	ch	sh	r
o					X	X	X	X	X	X	X	X	X	X	X	X	X	X
u																		
ou	X																	

❷ **u** is spelled wu when it stands alone.

COMBINING SOUNDS

Listen to the audio track. Practice pronunciation and tones.

p + o = po

pō pó pǒ pò

pōdù *n.* slope

○ Zhè tiáo lù pōdù zhēn dǒu.
This road is very steep.

f + u = fu

fū fú fǔ fù

fù *v.* to pay

○ Zhè běn shū nǐ yào fù wǔbǎi yuán.
You need to pay five hundred dollars for this book.

k + ou = kou

kōu kǒu kòu

shùkǒu *v.* to rinse the mouth

○ Chī wán fàn zuìhǎo shuāyá shùkǒu.
It's better to gargle and brush your teeth after having a meal.

h + u = hu

hū hú hǔ hù

lǎohǔ *n.* tiger

○ Zhège dòngwùyuán lǐ yǒu liǎng zhī lǎohǔ.
There are two tigers in this zoo.

READ OUT LOUD

pó / pú / póu   mǒ / mǔ / mǒu   fó / fú / fǒu   dù / dòu

hǔ / hǒu   zū / zōu / zhū / zhōu   sù / sòu / shù / shòu

SPEAK AND SING

Shāntóu yǒu lǎohǔ, sēnlín yǒu huālù,

lùbiān yǒu xiǎozhū, cǎolǐ yǒu báitù,

hòuyuàn yǒu huīshǔ. Qǐng nǐ shǔ yì shǔ,

Yī、èr、sān、sì、wǔ, hǔ、lù、zhū、tù、shǔ.

En   There is a tiger on the mountaintop. There is a deer in the forest.
There is a pig on the roadside. There is a rabbit in the grass.
There is a mouse in the backyard. Please count with your fingers.
One, two, three, four, five! There is a tiger, a deer, a pig, a rabbit, and a mouse.

PRACTICAL SENTENCES

Nǐ jia yǒu jǐ kǒu rén?

How many people are there in your family?

GIVE IT A TRY

 Track 56

Part 1 Listen to the audio track. Circle the picture of the word that uses the final on the left.

Part 2 Write the finals you hear from the audio track.

(Note: Tones can be disregarded for this exercise.)

Ex. xiaot _ou_

❶ pif_____ ❷ dal_____ ❸ lao p_____ p_____

Part 3 Listen to the audio track. Circle the correct one.

Ex.	❶	❷	❸
bū	dū	lōu	bō
bú	dú	lóu	bó
bǔ	dǔ	lǒu	bǒ
(bù)	dù	lòu	bò

UNIT 11

b p m f d t n l g k h z

c s zh ch sh r

+ e ei

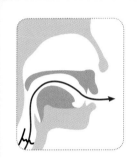

❶ Open your mouth half-wide. At the same time, spread your lips apart, as if you were smiling.

❷ as in *lotus* (but the position is rear)

....

Ex hé *n.* river

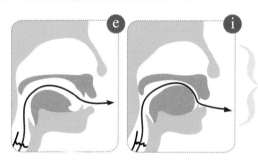

❶ **ei** consists of **e** and **i**. To pronounce **ei**, say **e** first. Then make your mouth flat to say **i**.

❷ as in *eight*

....

Ex bēi *n. / m.* cup

💡 NOTES

The following finals do not combine with the following initials:

Finals \ Initials	b	p	m	f	d	t	n	l	g	k	z	h	c	s	zh	ch	sh	r
e	X	X		X														
ei				X					X					X		X		X

74

COMBINING SOUNDS

Listen to the audio track. Practice pronunciation and tones.

h + e = he

hē hé hè

hē *v.* to drink

○ Xiūxi yíxià hē bēi shuǐ.
Take a break and drink a cup of water.

l + e = le

lē lè

kuàilè *sv.* to be happy

○ Chànggē ràng rén hěn kuàilè.
Singing makes people happy.

f + ei = fei

fēi féi fěi fèi

fēijī *n.* airplane

○ Wǒmen zuò fēijī qù Déguó.
We went to Germany by plane.

g + ei = gei

gěi

gěi *v.* to give
prep. for

○ Zhè shì sòng gěi nǐ de lǐwù.
This is a present for you.

UNIT
11

 **READ OUT LOUD**

dć / děi   nè / nèi   gě / gěi   hē / hēi   nè / lè / rè

gē / kē / hē   zè / zhè   sè / shè   bèi / pèi   nèi / lèi

 SPEAK AND SING

dāng hēiyè   láilín   xīng rú   fěicuì míng   nǐ de méi

rú   bèilěi   fēnfāng zài   wǒ   de xīnfēi   nǐ de xiào rú méigui

shèngkāi zài   wǒ   de kāfēibēi   xiǎng hé nǐ   yìqǐ   fēi

fēi   xiàng běifāng de   bǎolěi

En   When night comes, the stars are bright like emeralds. Your eyebows
      are like buds, perfume is in my heart. Your smile is like a rose,
      blooming in my coffee cup. I wish I could fly with you,
      to the bastion in the north.

 PRACTICAL SENTENCES

Qǐng gěi wǒ càidān.   The menu, please.

Qǐng gěi wǒ zhàngdān.   The bill, please.

 Track 61

GIVE IT A TRY

Part 1 Listen to the audio track. Circle the picture of the word that uses the final on the left.

Part 2 Write the finals you hear from the audio track.
(Note: Tones can be disregarded for this exercise.)

Ex. b ei z i

❶ k_____ai   ❷ k u a i l_____   ❸ h_____b a n

Part 3 Listen to the audio track. Circle the correct one.

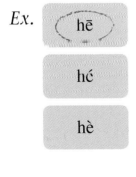

Ex.

| hē |
| hć |
| hè |

❶

| fēi |
| féi |
| fěi |
| fèi |

❷

| zhē |
| zhé |
| zhě |
| zhè |

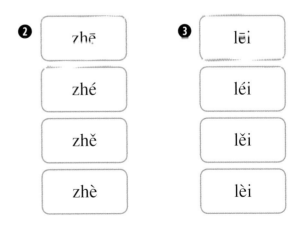

❸

| lēi |
| léi |
| lěi |
| lèi |

UNIT
11

77

UNIT 12

SIMPLE PINYIN SOUNDS

Track 62

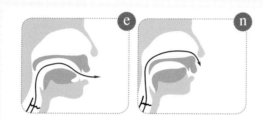

1 Keep your mouth flat to say **e** first. Then close it a bit to let the air out through the nasal cavity ending with **n**.

2 as in *bacon*

....

Ex hěn *adv.* very

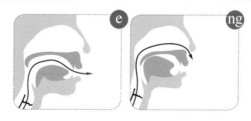

1 Keep your mouth flat to say **e** first. Then close it a bit to let the air out through the back part of the nasal cavity ending with **ng**.

2 as in *lung (but the mouth open smaller)*

....

Ex dēng *n.* light

NOTES

The final **en** does not combine with **t** and **l**.

COMBINING SOUNDS

Listen to the audio track. Practice pronunciation and tones.

b + en = ben

bēn běn bèn

běn *m.* measure word for books, notebooks, etc.

🔾 Wǒ xǐhuan zhè běn shū.
I like this book.

f + eng = feng

fēng féng fěng fèng

fēng *n.* wind

🔾 Jīntiān fēng hěn dà.
The wind today is very strong.

m + en = men

mēn mén mèn

mén *n.* door

🔾 Qǐng suíshǒu guān mén.
Please close the door behind you.

p + eng = peng

pēng péng pěng pèng

péngyou *n.* friend

🔾 Wǒmen shì hǎo péngyou.
We are good friends.

READ OUT LOUD

 Track 63

bēn / bēng   mèn / mèng   fēn / fēng   hén / héng

zhēn / zhēng   rén / réng   sēn / shēng

néng / léng / réng   cén / chén

 SPEAK AND SING

 Track 64

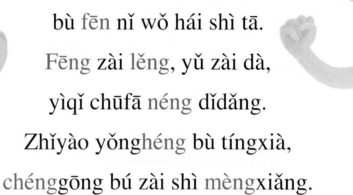

Péngyoumen, gēn wǒ lái,

bù fēn nǐ wǒ hái shì tā.

Fēng zài lěng, yǔ zài dà,

yìqǐ chūfā néng dǐdǎng.

Zhǐyào yǒnghéng bù tíngxià,

chénggōng bú zài shì mèngxiǎng.

En Friends, come with me.
That includes you, him, and me.
Although the wind is chilly, the rain is heavy.
Together, we can withstand them.
As long as we don't stop,
Success is no longer a dream.

 PRACTICAL SENTENCES

 Track 65

Zhè shì shénme?

What is this?

 **GIVE IT A TRY**

Part 1 Listen to the audio track. Circle the picture of the word that uses the final on the left.

Part 2 Write the finals you hear from the audio track.
(Note: Tones can be disregarded for this exercise.)

Ex. beif eng

❶ taid_____   ❷ t_____tong   ❸ g_____b_____

Part 3 Listen to the audio track. Circle the correct one.

Ex.
bēn

bèn

❶
dèng

děng

dèng

❷
hén

hěn

hèn

❸
gēng

gěng

gèng

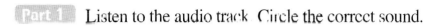

Part 1   Listen to the audio track. Circle the correct sound.   Track 67

Ex.

hū

hú

(hǔ)

1.

é

ě

è

2.

mēn

mén

mèn

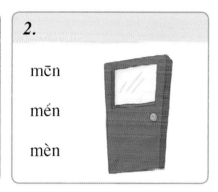

3.

léng

lěng

lèng

4.

kōu

kǒu

kòu

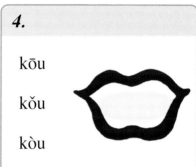

5.

féi

fěi

fèi

Part 2   Listen to the audio track. Fill in the missing initials and finals.

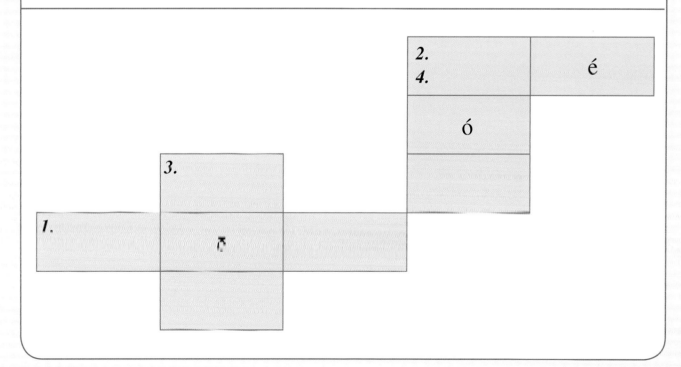

2.		é
4.		
	ó	

3.

1.

Listen the audio track. Choose the correct initials and finals from below.

(Note: Tones can be disregarded for this excrcise.)

❶ d ❷ p ❸ m ❹ g ❺ h ❻ ong ❼ ou ❽ u ❾ e ❿ ei

Ex. [1 , 9] **1.** [ ] **2.** [ ] .**3.** [ ] **4.** [ ]

Part 4 Listen to the audio track. Circle the correct finals.

Ex.

   o   (u)   ou

1.

   i   e   ei

2.

   en   cng

3.

   o   u   ou

4.

   en   eng

In this section, we will learn the finals beginning with **i**. We will also combine them with the following initials:

b p m f

d t n l

Then, we will learn three new initials, and combine with the –i finals:

UNIT
17

j q x +

i ia iao

ie iu ian in

iang ing iong

P. 102

b p m f d t n l

+ i ia iao

📖 SIMPLE PINYIN SOUNDS

 Track 68

ia

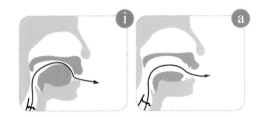

❶ Pronounce **i** first and then **a**.

❷ as in *yacht* (but open the mouth wider, and the tongue position is front)

Ex yā *n.* duck

iao

❶ Pronounce **i** first and then **ao**.

❷ as in *yowl* (but the tongue position is front)

Ex yào *n.* medication

💡 NOTES

❶ The final **l** and **iao** do not combine with **f**.

❷ The final **ia** does not combine with **b**, **p**, **m**, **f**, **d**, **t**, and **n**.

❸ -i finals can all stand by themselves. **i**, **ia**, and **iao** are spelled **yi**, **ya**, and **yao** when they stand alone.

COMBINING SOUNDS

Listen to the audio track. Practice pronunciation and tones.

b + i = bi
bī bí bǐ bì

gāngbǐ *n.* pen

○ Zhè zhī gāngbǐ hěn piàoliang.
   The pen is very beautiful.

i + a = ia
yā yá yǎ yà

yá *n.* teeth

○ Yáténg yào zhǎo yáyī zhì.
   You should go to see a dentist when you have a toothache.

b + iao = biao
biāo biǎo biào

shǒubiǎo *n.* watch

○ Wǒ yǒu yì zhī xīn shǒubiǎo.
   I have a new watch.

d + i = di
dī dí dǐ dì

dìfang *n.* place

○ Nǐ jiā zài shénme dìfang?
   Where is your home?

READ OUT LOUD

Track 69

yī / yā / yāo   lǐ / liǎ / liǎo   bí / pí

ní / lí   biāo / diāo   miǎo / niǎo   diào / tiào

SPEAK AND SING

Track 70

Lí jiā sòng Lǐ jiā lí, Lǐ jiā sòng Lí jiā lǐ.

Lǐ jiā qīzi chī lí bù tǔ pí, Lí jiā qīzi chī lǐ huì tǔ pí.

Lǐ jiā qīzi chīnìle lí, yào chī Lí jiā qīzi de lǐ;

Lí jiā qīzi chīnìle lǐ, yào chī Lǐ jiā qīzi de lí.

Lǐ jiā qīzi chī lǐ bù tǔ pí, Lí jiā qīzi chī lí huì tǔ pí.

En The Li family gives the Lee family pears as a gift;
The Lee family gives the Li family plums as a gift.
Mrs. Lee doesn't spit the peel when eating a pear;
Mrs. Li spits the peel when eating a plum.
Mrs. Lee is bored with pears and wants to eat Mrs. Li's plums;
Mrs. Li is bored with plums and wants to eat Mrs. Lee's pears.
Mrs. Lee doesn't spit the peel when eating a plum;
Mrs. Li also spits the peel when eating a pear.

PRACTICAL SENTENCES

Track 71

Wǒ yào kàn yīshēng.

I need to see a doctor.

GIVE IT A TRY

Track 72

Part 1   Listen to the audio track. Write down the correct finals.

Ex. lóut_ī_

❶ shǒub_____   ❷ d_____bǎn   ❸ _____zhōu

Part 2   Listen to the audio track. Circle the correct one.

Ex.

diāo

diǎo

(diào)

❶	❷	❸
mī	yā	miāo
mí	yá	miáo
mǐ	yǎ	miǎo
mì	yà	miào

Part 3   Listen to the audio track. Then write down their phonetic

Ex. yā   ❶ _____   ❷ _____

❸ _____   ❹ _____   ❺ _____

89

UNIT 14

SIMPLE PINYIN SOUNDS

Track 73

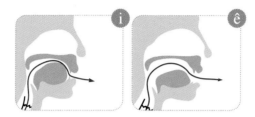

❶ Pronounce **i** first and then **ê**.

❷ as in *yellow*

....

Ex **yè** *n.* night

❶ Pronounce **i** first and then **ou**.

❷ as in *yoke*

....

Ex **yǒu** *v.* to have

NOTES

❶ The final **ie** does not combine with **f**.

❷ The final **iou** does not combine with **b**, **p**, **f**, and **t**.

❸ **ie** and **iou** are spelled **ye** and **you** when they stand alone. When an initial is added before **iou**, it is written as **iu**. For example, **niú** (cow).

COMBINING SOUNDS

Listen to the audio track. Practice pronunciation and tones.

i + ê = ie

yē yé yě yè

yéye *n.* grandfather

○ Wǒ bāng yéye xǐ diézi.
I helped my grandfather wash dishes.

i + ou = iou

yōu yóu yǒu yòu

yóuyǒng *v.* to swim

○ Yè xiǎojiě hé péngyou qù yóuyǒng.
Miss Ye went swimming with her friend.

d + ie = die

diē dié

diē *v.* to fall down

○ Tā zài mén qián diēle yì jiāo.
She fell in front of the door.

l + iu = liu

liū liú liǔ liù

liú *v.* to leave

○ Dìdi liú gěi wǒ yí kuài liúliángāo.
My younger brother left me a piece of durian cake.

READ OUT LOUD

yě / yǒu   miè / miù   niē / niū   liè / liù

tè / tiè   lè / liè   dōu / diū   lóu / liú

SPEAK AND SING

Diēdie sòng wǒ jīnsīchóu, māma sòng wǒ dà huángniú,

gēge sòng wǒ báiliǔshàn, jiějie sòng wǒ xiǎo liègǒu.

Chuānle chóu, qíle niú, báiliǔshàn, zhē rìtou,

Hòutou hái gēnle ge xiǎo liègǒu.

En Father gives me some golden silk; Mother gives me a big cow.
Elder brother gives me a white willow fan;
Elder sister gives me a little retriever.
I wear the golden silk coat, ride the cow,
Take the white willow fan to block the sunshine,
And I'm followed by a little retriever.

PRACTICAL SENTENCES

Fùjìn yǒu yóujú ma?   Is there a post office nearby?

Fùjìn yǒu yīyuàn ma?   Is there a hospital nearby?

GIVE IT A TRY

Part 1 Listen to the audio track. Write down the correct finals.

Ex. _yē_ zi

❶ q_____ zi   ❷ d_____diào   ❸ n_____ y_____

Part 2 Listen to the audio track. Circle the correct one.

Ex.

(biē)	❶ tiē	❷ yōu	❸ liū
bié	tiě	yóu	liú
biě	tiè	yǒu	liǔ
biè		yòu	liù

Part 3 Listen to the audio track. Then write down their phonetic

Ex. _yè_   ❶ _____   ❷ _____

❸ _____   ❹ _____   ❺ _____

UNIT 15

b p m f d t n l

+ ian iang

ian

❶ Pronounce **i** first and then **an**.

❷ as in *little* plus **an**

....

Ex yán *n.* salt

iang

❶ Pronounce **i** first and then **ang**.

❷ as in *little* plus **ang**

....

Ex yáng *n.* goat

NOTES

❶ The following finals do not combine with the following initials:

Initials Finals	b	p	m	f	d	t	n	l
ian				X				
iang	X	X	X	X	X	X		

❷ **ian** and **iang** are spelled **yan** and **yang** when they stand alone.

COMBINING SOUNDS

Listen to the audio track. Practice pronunciation and tones.

i + an = ian

yān yán yǎn yàn

yǎnjing *n.* eyes

○ Tián xiǎojiě yǒu yì shuāng měilì de yǎnjing.
Miss Tian has beautiful eyes.

i + ang = iang

yāng yáng yǎng yàng

yàngzi *n.* appearance, shape, type of

○ Zhè jiàn yīfu de yàngzi hěn hǎokàn.
The style of the clothes is very beautiful.

l + ian = lian

lián liǎn liàn

xiàoliǎn *n.* smiling face

○ Tā zǒngshi xiàoliǎn yíng rén
He always smiles at everyone.

n + iang = niang

niáng niàng

gūniang *n.* girl

○ Nàge gūniang piàoliang yòu shànliáng.
That girl is pretty and kind-hearted.

READ OUT LOUD

Track 79

nán / nián / niáng   làn / liàn / liàng   bān / biān

tǎn / tiǎn   biàn / piàn   mián / nián

diān / tiān   niàng / liàng

SPEAK AND SING

Track 80

hǎo xiǎng nǐ hǎo xiǎng nǐ   měitiān xiǎng nǐ hǎo jǐ biàn

nǐ de liǎn hé   nǐ de xiào   diǎndiǎndīdī   zài xīnjiān hǎo

xiǎng nǐ   hǎo xiǎng nǐ   hǎo xiǎng hé nǐ   jiàn yí miàn

kuài lái jìnrù   wǒ mèng zhōng   liǎng rén xiāngyī   yòu xiāngwēi

En   Miss you. Miss you. I miss you all the time.
Your face and your smile are always on my mind.
Miss you. Miss you. I want to see you in front of me.
Please come into my dream. Let's nestle together.

PRACTICAL SENTENCES

Track 81

Xiànzài jǐ diǎn?

What time is it now?

 GIVE IT A TRY

Track 82

Part 1 Listen to the audio track. Write down the correct finals.

Ex. t iān kōng

❶ niúròum_____   ❷ x_____y_ ___   ❸ wǔ d___

Part 2 Listen to the audio track. Circle the correct one.

Ex.   liáng

liǎng

(liàng)

❶
biān

biǎn

biàn

❷
yāng

yáng

yǎng

yàng

❸
niān

nián

niǎn

niàn

Part 3 Listen to the audio track. Then write down their phonetic

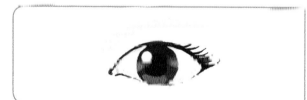

Ex. yǎn   ❶_____

❷_____   ❸_____

UNIT 16

b p m f d t n l

+ in ing

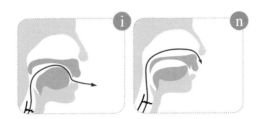

❶ Pronounce **i** first and then **n**.

❷ as in *in*

Ex yín   *n.*   silver

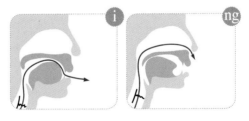

❶ Pronounce **i** first and then **ng**.

❷ as in *king*

Ex yīng   *n.*   infant

NOTES

❶ The final **in** does not combine with **f**, **d**, and **t**.

❷ The final **ing** does not combine with **f**.

❸ **in** and **ing** are spelled **yin** and **ying** when they stand alone.

COMBINING SOUNDS

Listen to the audio track. Practice pronunciation and tones.

i + n = in

yīn yín yǐn yìn

yīn**yuè** *n.* music

○ Wǒ xǐhuan tīng liúxíng yīnyuè.
I like to listen to pop music.

i + ng = ing

yīng yíng yǐng yìng

Yīng**wén** *n.* English language

○ Wǒ mǎile liǎng běn Yīngwén shū.
I bought two English books.

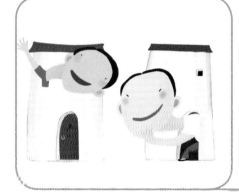

l + in = lin

līn lín lǐn lìn

lín**jū** *n.* neighbor

○ Lín xiānsheng shì wǒ de línjū.
Mr. Lin is my neighbor.

m + ing = ming

míng mǐng mìng

míng**piàn** *n.* business card

○ Wáng xiānsheng hé wǒ hùxiāng jiāohuàn míngpiàn.
Mr. Wang and I exchanged business cards with each other.

🐦 READ OUT LOUD

🎧 Track 84

yìn / yìng   bīn / bīng   pīn / pīng

mín / míng   nín / níng   lìn / lìng

bìn / pìn   dīng / tīng   nín / lín   míng / níng

🌐 SPEAK AND SING

🎧 Track 85

(In a formal meeting)

A Nín hǎo! Wǒ jiào Dīng Xiǎopíng.
Qǐngwèn nín guìxìng?

B Nín hǎo! Bìxìng Lín.
Wǒ de míngzi shì Lín Dàmín.

A Zhè shì wǒ de míngpiàn.
Qǐng duōduō zhǐjiào.

B Zhè shì wǒ de míngpiàn.
Hěn gāoxìng rènshi nín.

En A: Hi! I am Xiaopin Ding. May I ask what your last name is?
B: Hi! My last name is Lin. My full name is Damin Lin.
A: This is my business card. Great to meet you.
B: This is my business card. Nice to meet you.

🌐 PRACTICAL SENTENCES

🎧 Track 86

Nǐ jiào shénme míngzi?

What is your name?

 **GIVE IT A TRY** Track 87

Part 1 Listen to the audio track. Write down the correct finals.

Ex. sēnl ín

❶ d_____zi   ❷ y_____háng   ❸ p_____ān

Part 2 Listen to the audio track. Circle the correct one.

Ex.

(xīn)

xín

xìn

❶ līng / líng / lǐng / lìng

❷ qīng / qíng / qǐng / qìng

❸ pīn / pín / pǐn / pìn

Part 3 Listen to the audio track. Then write down their phonetic

Ex. pín   ❶ _____

❷ _____   ❸ _____

101

📖 SIMPLE PINYIN SOUNDS

Track 88

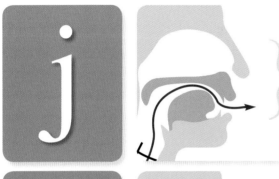

❶ Raise the front of your tongue to the hard palate and press the tip against the back of the lower teeth. Then squeeze air out through the channel formed. This sound is not aspirated.

❷ as in *genius*

Ex jī *n.* chicken

❶ As with **j**, raise the front of your tongue to the hard palate and press the tip against the back of the lower teeth. Then let the air out, only with a stronger breath. This sound is aspirated.

❷ as in *cheap*

Ex qī *nu.* seven

❶ Raise the front of your tongue toward the hard palate. Then let the air flow out through the channel formed between your tongue and hard palate.

❷ between *see* and *she* (tongue position as for **j**)

Ex xī *n.* west

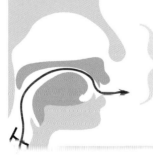

❶ Pronounce **i** first and then **ong**.

❷ as in *machine* with an **ong** around.

Ex yòng *v.* to use

COMBINING SOUNDS

Listen to the audio track. Practice pronunciation and tones.

j + ia = jia

jiā jiá jiǎ jià

jiā *n.* home, family

○ Wǒ jiā yǒu jiǔ kǒu rén.
There are nine people in my family.

q + i = qi

qī qí qǐ qì

qī *nu.* seven

○ Yí ge xīngqī yǒu qī tiān.
There are seven days in a week.

x + ie = xie

xiē xié xiě xiè

xiézi *n.* shoes

○ Qiū tàitai mǎile yì shuang xīn xiézi.
Mrs. Chiu bought a new pair of shoes.

q + iu = qiu

qiū qiú qiǔ

qiūtiān *n.* autumn, fall

○ Yì nián yǒu chūntiān、 xiàtiān、 qiūtiān hé dōngtiān.
There are spring, summer, fall, and winter in a year.

UNIT 17

READ OUT LOUD

Track 89

jié / qié / xié   jìn / qìn / xìn   jiū / qiū / xiū

jiǎo / qiǎo / xiǎo   jiǎn / qiǎn / xiǎn   jiàng / qiàng / xiàng

jī / zī / zhī   qí / cí / chí   xì / sì / shì

SPEAK AND SING

Track 90

Nǐ wèn wǒ de ài duō shēn,

qǐng nǐ shǔshu tiānshàng xīng.

Qīshí? Qībǎi? Qīqiān kē?

Tiānshàng xīngxing wú qióngjìn,

jiù xiàng wǒ duì nǐ de qíng,

wú biān wú jìn nán jìliàng.

En   You asked me how much I love you.
Please count how many stars there are in the sky.
Seventy? Seven hundred? Or seven thousand?
The stars in the sky are countless.
Just like my affection for you,
It is boundless and infinite.

PRACTICAL SENTENCES

Track 91

Zhège duōshǎo qián?

How much is this one?

 **GIVE IT A TRY**

 Track 92

Part 1 Listen to the audio track. Write down the correct finals.

Ex. tiānq ì

❶ píng_____ ❷ x_____x_____ ❸ x_____q _____y_____y_____

Part 2 Listen to the audio track. Circle the correct one.

Ex. (jiā)

❶
| xiāng |
| xiáng |
| xiǎng |
| xiàng |

❷
| qiān |
| qián |
| qiǎn |
| qiàn |

❸
| jiē |
| jié |
| jiě |
| jiè |

jiá

jiǎ

jià

Part 3 Listen to the audio track. Then write down their phonetic

Ex. jī ❶_____ _____ ❷_____

❸_____ ❹_____ ❺_____

Track 93

Part 1 Listen to the audio track. Circle the correct sound.

Ex.

yā
(yá)
yǎ

1.

yé
yě
yè

2.

yáng
yǎng
yàng

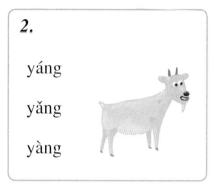

3.

yōu
yóu
yòu

4.

līn
lín
lǐn

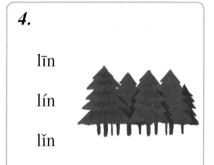

5.

xiā
xiá
xià

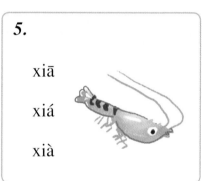

Part 2 Listen to the audio track. Fill in the missing initials and finals.

4.

à

3.

2.

ǎ

ǎ

1.

ī

106

Part 3 Listen to the audio track. Choose the correct initials and finals from below.
(Note: Tones can be disregarded for this exercise.)

① y **②** x **③** p **④** t **⑤** n **⑥** a **⑦** iao **⑧** iang **⑨** ian **⑩** in

Ex. | 4 , 9 | *1.* | | *2.* | | *3.* | | *4.* | |

Part 4 Crack the code to figure out the message.

Pinyin	∗	&	◎	#	=	□	Ω	×	π	α	β
	an	yi	ian	iu	ou	l	m	n	r	q	w

Tones		1		2		3		4
		—		╱		✓		╲

Code	&4	β∗3	×#2	π=4	Ω◎4	□#4	α◎1	□#4

Message | | | | | | | |

REVIEW ⑤

In this section, we will learn the finals beginning with **u**. We will also combine the finals with the initials shown below:

-u Finals

UNIT 18

b p m f d t
n l g k h z
c s zh ch sh r

+ u ua uo

P. 110

UNIT 19

d t g k h z
c s zh ch sh r

+ uai ui

P. 114

UNIT
20

d t n l g k

h z c s zh ch

sh r

+ uan uang   P. 118

UNIT
21

d t n l g k

h z c s zh ch

sh r

+ un ueng ong   P. 122

UNIT 18

b	p	m	f	d	t	n	l	g

k	h	z	c	s	zh	ch	sh	r

+ | u | ua | uo |

Track 94

📖 **SIMPLE PINYIN SOUNDS**

❶ Pronounce **u** first and then **a**.

❷ as in *watt*

······································

Ex wā *v.* to dig

❶ Pronounce **u** first and then **o**.

❷ as in *blue* plus **o**

······································

Ex wǒ *pron.* I; me

🌐 **NOTES**

❶ The final **ua** does not combine with **b, p, m, f, d, t, n, l, z, c, s**, and **r**.

❷ The final **uo** does not combine with **b, p, m**, and **f**.

❸ **-u** finals can all occur by themselves. **u, ua**, and **uo** are spelled **wu, wa**, and **wo** when they stand alone.

COMBINING SOUNDS

Listen to the audio track. Practice pronunciation and tones.

k + u = ku

kū kǔ kù

kū *v.* to cry

- Nàge xiǎohái yìzhí zài kū.
  That child keeps crying.

h + ua = hua

huā huá huà

huà *n.* painting
  v. to paint, to draw

- Hěn duō rén bù dǒng Bìjiāsuǒ de huà.
  Many people can not understand Picasso's paintings.

d + uo = duo

duō duó duǒ duò

duō *sv.* many, more

- Tiānshàng de xīngxing duō de shǔ bùqīng.
  The stars in the sky are countless.

zh + uo = zhuo

zhuō zhuó

zhuōzi *n.* table

- Nǐ de bǐ zài nàzhāng zhuōzi shàng.
  Your pen is on the table.

 **READ OUT LOUD**   Track 95

tú / tuó   lù / luò   gū / guā / guō   hù / huà / huò

sū / suō   zhū / zhuā / zhuō

 SPEAK AND SING   Track 96

Zhuōzi shàngfāng yǒu zhāng huà,

huàlǐ yǒu zhī dà luòtuo,

luòtuo bèishàng yǒu gūniang,

gūniang shǒushàng yǒu duǒ huā,

hái yǒu yì zhī xiǎo wōniú.

 En   There is a painting above the table.
There is a big camel in the painting.
There is a girl riding the camel.
The girl is holding a flower,
And a little snail.

 PRACTICAL SENTENCES   Track 97

Nǐ de diànhuà hàomǎ shì duōshǎo?

What is your phone number?

GIVE IT A TRY

Part 1 Listen to the audio track. Write down the correct finals.

Ex. n<u>ǚ</u>li

❶ l____bo   ❷ f____m____   ❸ h____píng

Part 2 Listen to the audio track. Circle the correct one.

Ex. (huā)   ❶ tū   ❷ kuā   ❸ duō

huá   tú   kuǎ   duó

huà   tǔ   kuà   duǒ

tù   duò

Part 3 Listen to the audio track. Then write down their phonetic

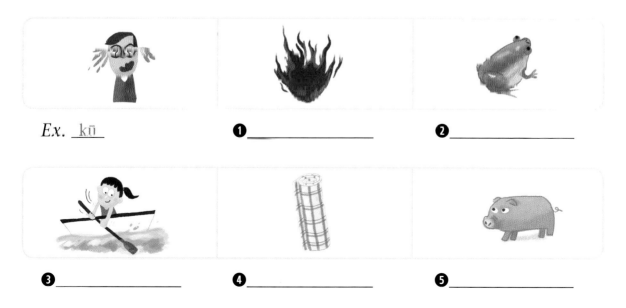

Ex. _kū_   ❶ _____   ❷ _____

❸ _____   ❹ _____   ❺ _____

d t g k h z c

s zh ch sh r

+ uai ui

📖 SIMPLE PINYIN SOUNDS

🎧 Track 99

uai

❶ Pronounce **u** first and then **ai**.

❷ as in *wife*

. . . .

Ex **wāi** *sv.* to be curved

ui

❶ Pronounce **u** first and then **ei**.

❷ as in *way*

. . . .

Ex **wèi** *n.* taste

💭 NOTES

❶ The following finals do not combine with the following initials:

Finals \ Initials	d	t	g	k	h	z	c	s	zh	ch	sh	r
uai	X	X				X	X	X				X
ui												

❷ **uai** and **ui** are spelled **wai** and **wei** when they stand alone. When an initial is added before **uei**, it is written as **ui**. For example, **duì** (correct).

COMBINING SOUNDS

Listen to the audio track. Practice pronunciation and tones.

u + ai = uai
wāi wǎi wài

wàimian   *n.*   outside

○ Màikè zài fángzi wàimian dǎsǎo.
Michael is cleaning outside the house.

u + ei = ui
wēi wéi wěi wèi

wéijīn   *n.*   scarf

○ Zhè tiáo wéijīn fēicháng guì.
The scarf is very expensive.

g + uai = guai
guāi guǎi guài

guāi   *sv.*   to be well-behaved

○ Tā shì ge hěn guāi de háizi.
He is a well-behaved child.

h + ui = hui
huī huí huǐ huì

huí   *v.*   to return

○ Lǎobǎn gǎn huí gōngsī kāihuì.
The boss hurried back to the office to hold a meeting.

READ OUT LOUD

guǎi / guǐ   kuài / kuì   huái / huí   shuǎi / shuǐ

guài / kuài / huài   duì / tuì   zhuī / chuī

SPEAK AND SING

En Winds blow lightly, and blow the flowers off the tree.
Flowers fly everywhere, till they fall on the clear lake.
The color of the lake is crystal green. The scenery of spring is beautiful.
Winds blow lightly. My baby is falling asleep.

PRACTICAL SENTENCES

Duìbùqǐ.

Sorry. / Excuse me.

GIVE IT A TRY

Part 1 Listen to the audio track. Write down the correct finals.

Ex. qíg <u>uài</u>

❶ sh___h_____   ❷ w_____w_____   ❸ k_____k_____sh_____

Part 2 Listen to the audio track. Circle the correct one.

Ex.

	❶	❷	❸
huī	shuāi	suī	guāi
(huí)	shuǎi	suí	guǎi
huǐ	shuài	suǐ	guài
huì		suì	

Part 3 Listen to the audio track. Then write down their phonetic

Ex. <u>tuǐ</u>   ❶ _____

❷ _____   ❸ _____

d t n l g k h z

c s zh ch sh r

+ uan uang

📖 **SIMPLE PINYIN SOUNDS**

uan

Pronounce **u** first and then **an**.

Ex wǎn *n.* bowl

uang

Pronounce **u** first and then **ang**.

Ex wàng *v.* to forget

🔄 **NOTES**

① The following finals do not combine with the following initials:

Finals \ Initials	d	t	n	l	g	k	h	z	c	s	zh	ch	sh	r
uan														
uang	✗	✗	✗	✗				✗	✗	✗				✗

② **uan** and **uang** are spelled **wan** and **wang** when they stand alone.

COMBINING SOUNDS

Listen to the audio track. Practice pronunciation and tones.

u + an = uan

wān wán wǎn wàn

wǎn**shàng**   *t.*   night

○ Wǒ zuótiān wǎnshàng qī diǎn chī wǎnfàn.
I had dinner at seven o'clock last night.

u + ang = uang

wāng wáng wǎng wàng

shàngwǎng   *v.*   to surf the internet

○ Wáng xiānsheng dào wǎngbā shàngwǎng.
Mr. Wang went to the Internet cafe to surf the Net.

s + uan = suan

suān suàn

suān   *sv.*   to be sour

○ Zhè ke níngméng wèidào hǎo suān.
This lemon tastes very sour.

ch + uang = chuang

chuāng chuáng chuǎng chuàng

qǐchuáng   *v.*   to get up

○ Wǒ gēge měitiān zǎoshàng bā diǎn qǐchuáng.
My elder brother gets up at eight o'clock everyday.

READ OUT LOUD

guān / guāng   kuān / kuāng   huàn / huàng

zhuān / zhuāng   chuán / chuáng   tán / tuán

gǎn / guǎn   kàng / kuàng   zān / zuān   shǎng / shuǎng

SPEAK AND SING

zǎoshàng qǐchuáng dǎkāi chuāng   chuāngwài tiānqì hěn qínglǎng

xiǎoniǎo chéngshuāng zài gēchàng   huànshàng qīngsōng de fúzhuāng

dǎqǐ jīngshén zhēn qīngshuǎng   měihǎo shìjiè   chuǎng yì chuǎng

En I open the window when I get up in the morning. The weather outside is bright and clear.
Birds are singing in pairs. I put on casual clothing,
Lift my spirit and feel really refreshed. I'm ready to explore this wonderful world.

PRACTICAL SENTENCES

Nǎlǐ kěyǐ huàn língqián?   Where can I get change?

Nǎlǐ kěyǐ huàn wàibì?   Where can I exchange foreign currency?

GIVE IT A TRY

Part 1 Listen to the audio track. Write down the correct finals.

Ex. h_uān_ yíng

❶ ch_____dan   ❷ s_____zhàng   ❸ g_____g_____

Part 2 Listen to the audio track. Circle the correct one.

Ex.

	❶	❷	❸
wān	chuāng	guāng	duān
wán	chuáng	guǎng	duǎn
(wǎn)	chuǎng	guàng	duàn
wàn	chuàg		

Part 3 Listen to the audio track. Then write down their phonetic

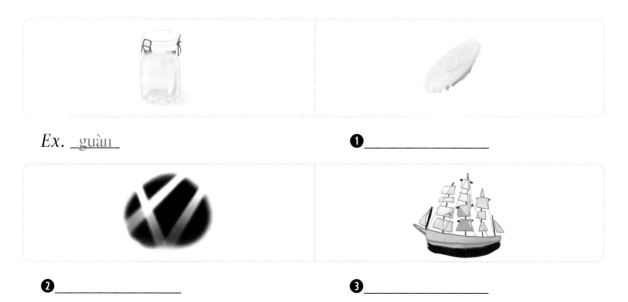

Ex. _guàn_   ❶_____

❷_____   ❸_____

121

d t n l g k h z

c s zh ch sh r

+ un ueng ong

SIMPLE PINYIN SOUNDS

 Track 109

un

1. Pronounce **u** first and then **en**.
2. as in *Owen*

....

Ex **wēn** *sv.* to be mildly warm

ueng

1. Pronounce **u** first and then **eng**.
2. Start with a **u** sound and end like *lung*.

....

Ex **wèng** *n.* earthen jar

ong

1. Pronounce **o** first and then **ng**.
2. as in *tone (but with the tongue back)*

....

Ex **hóng** *n.* red

NOTES

1. The final **un** does not combine with **n**. When an initial is added before **uen**, it is written as **un**. For example, **dūn** (squat). **un** is spelled **wen** when it stands alone.
2. **ueng** can only stand by itself, and it is spelled **weng**.
3. The final **ong** does not combine with **sh**.

COMBINING SOUNDS

Listen to the audio track. Practice pronunciation and tones.

u + en = uen

wēn wén wěn wèn

wèn'**an**   *v.*   to enquire after someone

○ Wǒ dǎ diànhuà xiàng fùmǔ wèn'ān.
I called my parents to see what they were doing.

u + eng = ueng

wēng wěng wèng

yú wēng   *n.*   old fisherman

○ Lǎo yú wēng zuì de liǎn hóngtōngtōng.
The old fisherman got drunk and turned bright red.

d + ong = dong

dōng dǒng dòng

dōng**bian**   *n.*   east

○ Wǒ jiā de dōngbian yǒu yí zuò shān.
There is a mountain on the east side of my house.

ch + un = chun

chūn chún chǔn

chūn**tiān**   *n.*   spring

○ Chūntiān shì wǒ zuì xǐhuan de jìjié.
Spring is my favorite season.

 **READ OUT LOUD**

tùn / tòng   kǔn / kǒng   zūn / zōng   chún / chóng

dōng / tōng   nóng / lóng   gùn / kùn / hùn

zūn / zhūn   sǔn / shǔn

 SPEAK AND SING

Nǐ huì dùn dòngdòufu, jiù dùn dòngdòufu;

rúguǒ nǐ búhuì dùn dòngdòufu, jiù bié dùn dòngdòufu.

Yàoshì nǐ jiǎzhuāng huì dùn dòngdòufu,

yídìng huì nònghuàile dùndòngdòufu,

nà jiù chī búdào nǐ de dùndòngdòufu.

En   If you know how to stew the frozen tofu,
Go ahead and stew the frozen tofu.
If you don't know how to stew the frozen tofu,
Please don't stew the frozen tofu.
If you pretend you can stew the frozen tofu,
You will ruin the frozen tofu.
Then you will not be able to eat the frozen tofu.

 PRACTICAL SENTENCES

Nǐ yǒu kòng ma?

Are you available?

GIVE IT A TRY

Track 113

Part 1   Listen to the audio track. Write down the correct finals.

Ex. jiéh ūn

❶ k_____qì   ❷ k_____ch_____   ❸ n_____rén

Part 2   Listen to the audio track. Circle the correct one.

Ex.

(tūn)   ❶ zhōng   ❷ sūn   ❸ dōng

tún   zhǒng   sǔn   dǒng

tǔn   zhòng   sùn   dòng

tùn

Part 3   Listen to the audio track. Then write down their phonetic

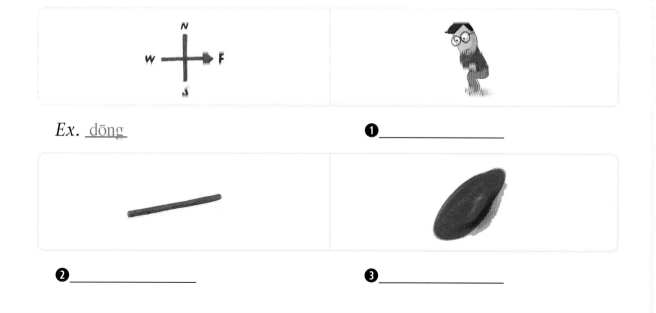

Ex. dōng   ❶ _____

❷ _____   ❸ _____

UNIT
21

125

Part 1   Listen to the audio track. Circle the correct sound.   Track 114

Ex.
wān
wán
(wǎn)

1.
huāng
huáng
huǎng
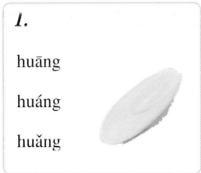

2.
hú
hǔ
hù
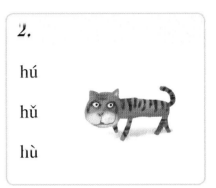

3.
guō
guó
guò
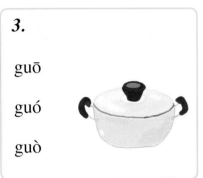

4.
huā
huá
huà

5.
chōng
chóng
chǒng
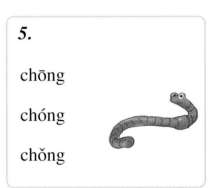

Part 2   Listen to the audio track. Fill in the missing initials and finals.

	3.			**4.**	
					ā
1.		á			g
	à				
2.		à			

Part 3 Listen the audio track. Choose the correct initials and finals from below.
(Note: Tones can be disregarded for this exercise.)

❶ d ❷ w ❸ g ❹ k ❺ h ❻ un ❼ ai ❽ u ❾ ui ❿ uo

Ex. 3 , 8   1. [　　]   2. [　　]   3. [　　]   4. [　　]

Part 4 Crack the code to figure out the message.

Pinyin	∗	&	◎	@	>	#	=	□	Ω	π	α	β	$
	h	m	i	ui	a	t	z	uan	uang	ei	x	ui	g

Tones	1	2	3	4	5
	–	╱	✓	╲	(netural tone)

Code   # >1   = @4   α ◎3   ∗ □5   ∗ Ω2   & π 2 $@5

Message   [　] [　]   [　　]   [　]   [　　]

REVIEW
⑥

In this section, we will learn the finals beginning with **ü**, and we will also combine the finals with the initials shown below:

-ü Finals

UNIT
22

j   q

x   n   l

+   ü   üe

P. 130

Finally, we will learn the final **er**, and how **er** combines with other finals to form a syllable with a retroflex ending.

UNIT 22

j q x n l + ü üe

SIMPLE PINYIN SOUNDS

 Track 115

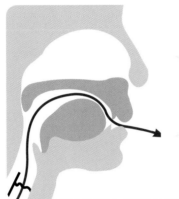

① First, pronounce **i**. Then, change the shape of your mouth from an un-rounded position to a rounded one.

② There is no English equivalent *(but it is similar to the beginning of the vowel sound in few)*

Ex yú *n.* fish

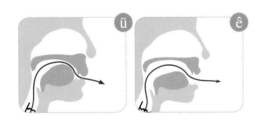

① Pronounce **ü** first and then **ê**. Change the shape of your mouth from a rounded position to a narrow one.

② There is no English equivalent *(but it is similar to the beginning of vowel sound in few, with an ê as in the group -i finals)*

Ex yuè *n.* moon

 NOTES

-ü finals can all stand by themselves. **ü** and **üe** are spelled **yu** and **yue** when they stand alone. Notice the two dots are removed. When **ü** and **üe** are spelled with **j**, **q**, or **x**, the two dots are also removed. When combining **ü** with **n** and **l**, we do not drop the dots. For example, we write **nǚ** (female).

COMBINING SOUNDS

Listen to the audio track. Practice pronunciation and tones.

n + ü = nü

nǔ nǜ

nǔhái *n.* girl

○ Nàge nǔhái hěn xǐhuan huáxuě.
That girl likes skiing very much.

ü + ê = üe

yuē yuě yuè

yuēhuì *v.* to date
n. a date

○ Lǚ xiǎojiě zhège Xīngqītiān yào hé nánpéngyou yuēhuì.
Miss Lu is going on a date with her boyfriend this Sunday.

l + ü = lü

lú lǔ lù

lǚxíng *v.* to travel

○ Zhège shǔjià wǒ xiǎng qù Zhōngguó lǚxíng.
I want to travel to China this summer vacation.

x + ue = xue

xuē xué xuě xuè

xuéxiào *n.* school

○ Wǒmen yìqǐ zǒulù qù xuéxiào.
We walked to school together.

Track 116

READ OUT LOUD

jú / jué   qū / quē   xù / xuè   nǚ / nüè   lǜ / lüè

jū / qū / xū   nǚ / lǚ   juè / què / xuè   nüè / lüè

SPEAK AND SING
Track 117

Qù lǚxíng, zhēn yǒuqù.

Kě chī jú, kě chī yú,

tīng yīnyuè, kàn huàjù.

Xiàqǐ yǔ lái zhēn yōuyù.

En Traveling is fun.
We can eat tangerines and fish,
Listen to music and watch plays.
It's melancholy when the rain comes.

PRACTICAL SENTENCES
Track 118

Wǒ xūyào yùyuē ma?

Do I need to make a reservation?

GIVE IT A TRY

Part 1 Listen to the audio track. Circle the correct one.

Ex. (jū)

jú

jǔ

jù

❶
juē
jué
juě
juè

❷
lǘ
lǚ
lǜ

❸
qūe
qúe
què

Part 2 Listen to the audio track. Circle the correct one.

Ex. (xùrì)

xūshí

xǔrì

❶
yuēqū
yuèqǔ
yuēxí

❷
quántou
yuāntou
xuāntou

❸
yǔyuè
yúyuè
yùyuē

❹
lǚxíng
nǔlín
nǔxù

Part 3 Listen to the audio track. Then write down their phonetic

Ex. _yuè_   ❶ _____

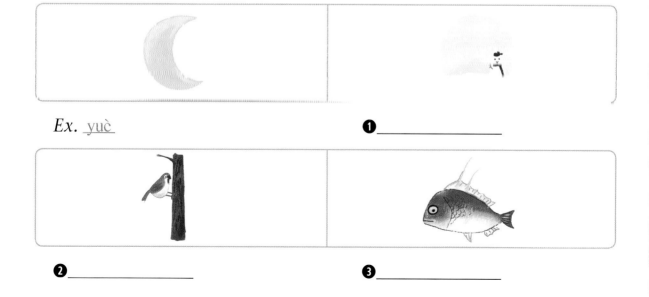

❷ _____   ❸ _____

UNIT 23

j q x
+ üan ün

SIMPLE PINYIN SOUNDS

1. Pronounce **ü** first and then **an**. Change the shape of your mouth from a round position to a narrow one.

2. There is no English equivalent *(but it is similar to the beginning of the vowel sound in few, with the **an** as in the group **-i** finals)*

Ex yuán *n.* round

1. Pronounce **ü** first and then **en**. The mouth shape changes from round to narrow.

2. There is no English equivalent *(but it is similar to the beginning of the vowel sound in few, and followed by a final **n**)*

Ex yún *n.* cloud

NOTES

1. When an initial is added before **üen**, it is written as **ün**. For example, **jùn** (handsome).

2. **üan** and **ün** are spelled **yuan** and **yun** when they stand alone. Notice the two dots are removed. When **üan** and **ün** are spelled with **j**, **q**, or **x**, the two dots are also removed.

COMBINING SOUNDS

Listen to the audio track. Practice pronunciation and tones.

ü + an = üan

yuān yuán yuǎn yuàn

yuǎn *sv.* to be far

○ Tā jiā lí wǒ jiā hěn yuǎn.
His house is far from my house.

ü + en = ün

yūn yún yǔn yùn

yùn**dòng** *v.* to exercise
n. exercise, sports

○ Xú xiānsheng zǎoqǐ qù yùndòng.
Mr. Xu gets up early to exercise.

x + uan = xuan

xuān xuán xuǎn xuàn

xuǎn *v.* to choose

○ Wǒ xuǎn zhège huāpíng sòng gěi tā.
I choose this vase to give her.

q + ün = qun

qūn qún

qún**zi** *n.* skirt

○ Ānnà qiántiān chuānle yí jiàn lánsè de qúnzi.
Anna wore a blue skirt the day before yesterday.

UNIT
23

 READ OUT LOUD

yūn / yuān   jùn / juàn   qún / quán   xūn / xuān

jūn / qūn / xūn   juàn / quàn / xuàn

 SPEAK AND SING

Diànshì yǎnyuán yǒu liǎng ge,

yí ge jiào Yuán yǎnyuán,

yí ge jiào Wēn yǎnyuán.

Yuán yǎnyuán tǎoyàn Wēn yǎnyuán,

Wēn yǎnyuán máiyuàn Yuán yǎnyuán.

En   There are two TV actors.
One is Yuan and the other is Wen.
Yuan dislikes Wen and Wen grumbles about Yuan.

 PRACTICAL SENTENCES

Zhù nǐ hǎoyùn!

Good luck to you!

 **GIVE IT A TRY**

Part 1 Listen to the audio track. Circle the correct one.

Ex. (xuān)   **❶** quān   **❷** xīn   **❸** juan

xuán   quán   xún   juǎn

xuǎn   quǎn   xùn   juàn

xuàn   quàn

Part 2 Listen to the audio track. Circle the correct one.

Ex. quǎnlí   **❶** jūnzǐ   **❷** qúnzì   **❸** lièquǎn   **❹** zhuìxūnxūn

(quánlì)   jūnzī   xùnzi   liěquán   zuìxūnxūn

quànlì   qúnshí   qúnzi   nièquǎn   zuìjūnjūn

Part 3 Listen to the audio track. Then write down their phonetic

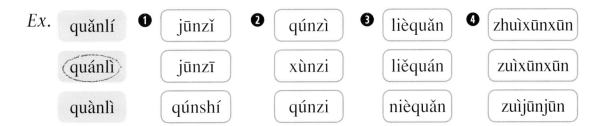

Ex. quǎn   **❶** _____

❷ _____   **❸** _____

UNIT
23

137

UNIT 24

Group -r Finals

📖 SIMPLE PINYIN SOUNDS

Track 125

 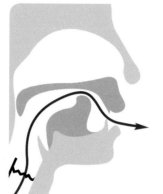

❶ Turn up the tip of your tongue toward the hard palate. Then let the air out with your tongue rolled.

❷ as in *rear*

Ex ér *n.* son

🔵 NOTES

❶ **er** can not follow an initial, but it can be used as a syllable. For example, **ér** (son) and **ěr** (ear).

❷ **er** can also combine with other finals to form a syllable with a retroflex ending. In the pinyin system, a retroflexed final is indicated by the letter **r** at the end of a syllable. When we write Chinese, we use the character 儿 (**ér**).

❸ **er** gives nouns a meaning of "small, lovely, or friendly." For example, when referring to **niǎo** (bird), we can also say **niǎo'er**.

138

COMBINING SOUNDS

Listen to the audio track. Practice pronunciation.

In spelling, add **r** directly after the final. Its actual pronunciation, however, changes in various ways:	◑ written ◐ pronounced	
• When combined with **a**, **ai**, **an**, **ang**, **ia**, **ian**, **iang**, **ua**, **uai**, **uan**, **uang** and **üan**, the **r** is sounded after the final **a**.	◑ wǎnr ◐ wǎr *n.* bowl	◑ huánr ◐ huár *n.* ring, loop
• When combined with **ei**, **en**, **eng**, **ie**, **üe**, **uei** and **uen**, the **r** is sounded after the final **e**.	◑ ménr ◐ mér *n.* door	◑ gùnr ◐ gùer *n.* rod, stick
• When combined with **i**, **in** and **ing**, the **er** is sounded after the final **i**.	◑ lír ◐ líer *n.* plum	
• When combined with **ü** and **ün**, the **er** is sounded after the final **ü**.	◑ yúr ◐ yuér *n.* fish	
• When combined with **zi**, **ci** and **si**, the **i** sound changes to **er**.	◑ zǐr ◐ zěr *n.* seed	
• When combined with **zhi**, **chi** and **shi**, the **i** sound changes to **er**	◑ zhǐr ◐ zhěr *n.* paper	
• When combined with **u**, **ou** and **iou**, the **r** is sounded after the final **u**.	◑ tùr ◐ tùr *n.* rabbit	
• When combined with **iong**, **ao**, **iao**, **uo** and **o**, the **r** is sounded after the final **o**.	◑ māor ◐ māor *n.* cat	◑ guōr ◐ guōr *n.* pot

UNIT
24

READ OUT LOUD

mǎr   huār   bāor   xiǎoháir   máolúr   guāzǐr

xiǎoxióngr   shítouzǐr   míngpáir   cháguǎnr

xìfǎr   méi shìr

SPEAK AND SING

In a restaurant

Fúwùyuán: Qǐngwèn sān wèi chī diǎnr shénme?

Xiānsheng: Gěi wǒ lái yìdiǎnr mápór dòufu.

Tàitai: Wǒ yào xiāngchángr liángbàn dòuyár.

Háizi: Wǒ yào chī jīdàn miàntiáor.

Fúwùyuán: Qǐng sān wèi shāo děng yíhuìr.

 En   Waiter / Waitress: Excuse me. What would you like to order?
Husband: I would like some mapo tofu.
Wife: I would like sausages with bean sprouts.
Kid: I would like egg noodles.
Waiter / Waitress: Please wait a moment.

PRACTICAL SENTENCES

Qǐng děng yíhuìr.

Please wait a moment.

 **GIVE IT A TRY**

Part 1 Write down the correct pinyin after adding the retroflexed final **er**.

Ex. xiǎomǎ → <u>xiǎomǎr</u>

❶ xiǎozhū → _____ ❷ shízi → _____

❸ nǎ → _____ ❹ yóupiào → _____

Part 2 Listen to the audio track. Circle the correct one.

Ex.

dǔjìr	❶ nár	❷ guāqúnr	❸ lǎobànr	❹ yùdiǎnr
(dùqír)	nǎr	huājùnr	lǎopànr	yǔdiǎnr
tùqír	nàr	huāqúnr	lǎobǎnr	yǔtiānr

Part 3 Listen to the audio track. Then write down their phonetic

Ex. <u>ménr</u>   ❶ _____

❷ _____   ❸ _____

Part 1 Listen to the audio track. Circle the correct sound. 🎧 Track 130

Ex.

jū

(jú)

jǔ

1.

xuē

xuć

xuě

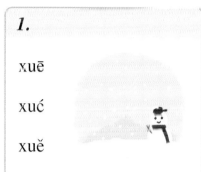

2.

yuān

yuán

yuàn

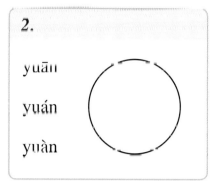

3.

quān

quán

quǎn

4.

yú

yǔ

yù

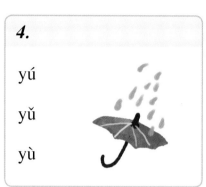

5.

yūn

yún

yùn

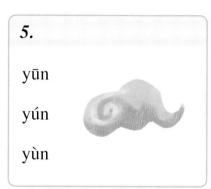

Part 2 Listen to the audio track. Fill in the missing initials and finals.

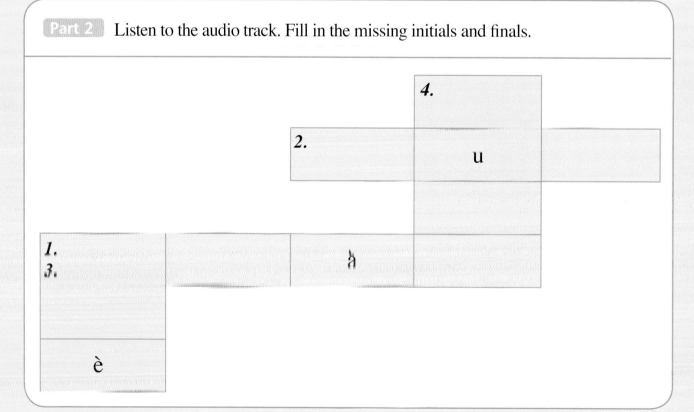

4.

2.

u

1.
3.

à

è

Listen to the audio track. Write down the correct final.

Ex. j<u>ù</u>

1. x_____ ____

2. n _____

3. q_____

4. l_____

5. w_____

6. g_____ __

Part 4 Listen to audio track. Circle the correct answer to complete the sentence.

Ex. Zhège zhōumò wǒ yào qù Xiānggǎng lǚyíng /(lǚxíng)/ jūnxíng.

1. Nàge yuánliǎn de nǚháir xǐhuan chuān qúnzi / jūnzi / qúnzhī .

2. Zhāng xiānsheng xǐhuan hē jǔhuà / jūhuá / júhuā chá .

3. Wǒ zuì xǐhuan tīng Bèiduōfēn de yuèqǔ / yùqǔ / yuèqì .

4. Niǔyuē de yīyuè zhèngzài xiàxiè / xiàxuě / xiàquè .

5. Tā quǎn / xuǎn / jiān yì tiáo zhēnzhū xiàngliàn sòng gěi nǚpéngyou.

En *Ex.* I will travel to Hong Kong this weekend.

1. That girl with round face likes to wear skirts.
2. Mr. Zhang likes to drink chrysanthemum tea.
3. I like to listen the Beethoven's compositions.
4. It's snowing in New York in January.
5. He chose a pearl necklace as a gift for his girlfriend.

REVIEW
⑦

Part 1   Comparison of **z, c, s** and **zh, ch, sh** initials:

❶	dà zì		big character
	dàzhì	*adv.*	approximately
❷	cìyào	*sv.*	secondary; less important
	chī yào	*v.*	to take medicine
❸	sān suì		three years old
	shānshuǐ	*n.*	mountains and waters
❹	zǔfù	*n.*	Grandfather
	zhǔfù	*n.*	housewife
❺	cū bù	*n.*	coarse cloth
	chūbù	*sv.*	initial

Part 2   Comparison of **n** and **ng** finals:

❶	chuán shàng		on the boat
	chuáng shàng		on the bed
❷	jīnyú	*n.*	goldfish
	jīngyú	*n.*	whale
❸	rénmín	*n.*	people
	rénmíng	*n.*	a person's name
❹	bú xìn		do not believe
	búxìng	*sv.*	to be unfortunate
❺	chūshēn	*n.*	family background
	chūshēng	*v.*	to be born

Part 3　Comparison of **i** and **ü** finals:

① yí cì　　　　　　　　　　　once
　 yúcì　　　　　*n.*　　　　fishbone

② qiántiān　　　*n.*　　　　the day before yesterday
　 quántian　　　*n.*　　　　whole day

③ yìjiàn　　　　*n.*　　　　opinion
　 yùjiàn　　　　*v.*　　　　to run across

④ yánliào　　　*n.*　　　　pigment
　 yuánliào　　 *n.*　　　　raw material

⑤ yànzi　　　　*n.*　　　　swallow
　 yuànzi　　　 *n.*　　　　yard

Part 4　Comparison of **l** and **n** finals:

① líba　　　　　*n.*　　　　fence
　 níba　　　　　*n.*　　　　mud

② lǎn rén　　　 *n.*　　　　lazy person
　 nánrén　　　 *n.*　　　　man

③ lākāi　　　　 *v.*　　　　to pull open
　 nákāi　　　　 *v.*　　　　to take away

④ lǚrén　　　　 *n.*　　　　traveler, wayfarer
　 nǚrén　　　　 *n.*　　　　woman

⑤ liúshuǐ　　　 *n.*　　　　running water
　 niúzuǐ　　　　*n.*　　　　cow's mouth

Every Chinese character has a constant pronunciation in pinyin. However, the pronunciation may change when we speak. Let's have a look at the rules and the examples below.

Part 1   The modulation of the 3rd tone

❶ A 3rd tone character keeps its original tone when it stands alone or is at the end of a word.

EX	hǎo	*sv.*	to be good
	jìnzhǐ	*v.*	to prohibit
	jīchǎng	*n.*	airport
	qìshuǐ	*n.*	soft drink

❷ When a 3rd tone character is followed by another 3rd tone character, the first character is pronounced in the 2nd tone. Despite the change in pronunciation, it is still written the same way in pinyin.

EX	shǒubiǎo → shóubiǎo	*n.*	watch
	cǎogǎo → cáogǎo	*n.*	draft
	lǎohǔ → láohǔ	*n.*	tiger
	yǔsǎn → yúsǎn	*n.*	umbrella

❸ When there are three 3rd tone characters coming in a row, the pronunciation changes according to the context. The two possible changes are [3rd -2nd -3rd] and [2nd -2nd -3rd].

ⓐ 3rd -2nd -3rd
   EX Milǎoshǔ → Miláoshǔ   *n.* Mickey mouse
      mǎi shuǐguǒ → mǎi shuíguǒ   *v.* to buy some fruit

ⓑ 2nd -2nd -3rd
   EX zhǎnlǎnguǎn → zhánlánguǎn *n.* exhibition center

Part 2　The modulation of 不 (bù)

❶ 不 (bù) is pronounced in the 4th tone when standing alone or preceding a syllable in the 1st, 2nd, and 3rd tones.

不 (bù) + 1st	bù chī	don't eat
	bù yīnggāi	should not
不 (bù) + 2nd	bù néng	can not
	bù huíjiā	do not go home
不 (bù) + 3rd	bù hǎo	not good
	bù měi	not beautiful

❷ 不 (bù) changes to the 2nd tone before a 4th tone character.

| Ex | bú shì | is not | | bú yào | do not want |
| | bú kèqi | You are welcome. | | | |

Part 3　The modulation of 一 (yī)

❶ 一 (yī) is pronounced in the 1st tone when standing alone or at the end of a syllable.

| Ex | shíyī | *nu.* | eleven | | dì-yī | first |

❷ 一 (yī) changes to the 4th tone when preceding a character in the 1st, 2nd, or 3rd tones.

一 (yī) + 1st	yì tiān	one day	(yī) + 2nd	yì nián	one year
	yì hé	one box		yì tiáo yú	a fish
一 (yī) + 3rd	yì diǎn	a little			
	yì běn shū	a book			

❸ 一 (yī) changes to the 2nd tone before a 4th tone character.

一 (yī)+4th	yí piàn	a piece of
	yídìng	sure
	yí cì	once

Finals		Simple Finals							Compound Finals				Nasal Finals				Retroflex	Group i Finals
		❶	❷	❸	❹	❺	❻	❼	❽	❾	❿	⓫	⓬	⓭	⓮	⓯	⓰	⓱
		a	o	e	ê	-i / yi	-u / wu	-ü / yu	ai	ei	ao	ou	an	en	ang	eng	er	-ia / ya
Initials																		
❶	b	ba	bo			bi	bu		bai	bei	bao		ban	ben	bang	beng		
❷	p	pa	po			pi	pu		pai	pei	pao	pou	pan	pen	pang	peng		
❸	m	ma	mo	me		mi	mu		mai	mei	mao	mou	man	men	mang	meng		
❹	f	fa	fo				fu			fei		fou	fan	fen	fang	feng		
❺	d	da		de		di	du		dai	dei	dao	dou	dan	den	dang	deng		
❻	t	ta		te		ti	tu		tai		tao	tou	tan		tang	teng		
❼	n	na		ne		ni	nu	nü	nai	nei	nao	nou	nan	nen	nang	neng		
❽	l	la		le		li	lu	lü	lai	lei	lao	lou	lan		lang	leng		lia
❾	g	ga		ge			gu		gai	gei	gao	gou	gan	gen	gang	geng		
❿	k	ka		ke			ku		kai		kao	kou	kan	ken	kang	keng		
⓫	h	ha		he			hu		hai	hei	hao	hou	han	hen	hang	heng		
⓬	j					ji		ju										jia
⓭	q					qi		qu										qia
⓮	x					xi		xu										xia
⓯	zh(i)	zha		zhe			zhu		zhai	zhei	zhao	zhou	zhan	zhen	zhang	zheng		
⓰	ch(i)	cha		che			chu		chai		chao	chou	chan	chen	chang	cheng		
⓱	sh(i)	sha		she			shu		shai	shei	shao	shou	shan	shen	shang	sheng		
⓲	r(i)			re			ru				rao	rou	ran	ren	rang	reng		
⓳	z(i)	za		ze			zu		zai	zei	zao	zou	zan	zen	zang	zeng		
⓴	c(i)	ca		ce			cu		cai	cei	cao	cou	can	cen	cang	ceng		
㉑	s(i)	sa		se			su		sai		sao	sou	san	sen	sang	seng		
Initials		a	o	e	ê	-i / yi	-u / wu	-ü / yu	ai	ei	ao	ou	an	en	ang	eng	er	-ia / ya
		❶	❷	❸	❹	❺	❻	❼	❽	❾	❿	⓫	⓬	⓭	⓮	⓯	⓰	⓱
Finals		Simple Finals							Compound Finals				Nasal Finals				Retroflex	Group i Finals

	Group i Finals							Group u Finals								Group ü Finals			
	⑱	⑲	⑳	㉑	㉒	㉓	㉔	㉕	㉖	㉗	㉘	㉙	㉚	㉛	㉜	㉝	㉞	㉟	㊱
	-ie	-iao	-iu	-ian	-in	-iang	-ing	-ua	-uo	-uai	-ui	-uan	-un	-uang	-ong	-üe	-üan	-ün	-iong
	ye	yao	you	yan	yin	yang	ying	wa	wo	wai	wei	wan	wen	wang	weng	yue	yuan	yun	yong
❶	bie	biao		bian	bin		bing												
❷	pie	piao		pian	pin		ping												
❸	mie	miao	miu	mian	min		ming												
❹																			
❺	die	diao	diu	dian			ding		duo		dui	duan	dun		dong				
❻	tie	tiao		tian			ting		tuo		tui	tuan	tun		tong				
❼	nie	niao	niu	nian	nin	niang	ning		nuo			nuan			nong	nüe			
❽	lie	liao	liu	lian	lin	liang	ling		luo			luan	lun		long	lüe			
❾								gua	guo	guai	gui	guan	gun	guang	gong				
❿								kua	kuo	kuai	kui	kuan	kun	kuang	kong				
⓫								hua	huo	huai	hui	huan	hun	huang	hong				
⓬	jie	jiao	jiu	jian	jin	jiang	jing									jue	juan	jun	jiong
⓭	qie	qiao	qiu	qian	qin	qiang	qing									que	quan	qun	qiong
⓮	xie	xiao	xiu	xian	xin	xiang	xing									xue	xuan	xun	xiong
⓯								zhua	zhuo	zhuai	zhui	zhuan	zhun	zhuang	zhong				
⓰								chua	chuo	chuai	chui	chuan	chun	chuang	chong				
⓱								shua	shuo	shuai	shui	shuan	shun	shuang					
⓲									ruo		rui	ruan	run		rong				
⓳									zuo		zui	zuan	zun		zong				
⓴									cuo		cui	cuan	cun		cong				
㉑									suo		sui	suan	sun		song				
	-ie	-iao	-iu	-ian	-in	-iang	-ing	-ua	-uo	-uai	-ui	-uan	-un	-uang	-ong	-üe	-üan	-ün	-iong
	ye	yao	you	yan	yin	yang	ying	wa	wo	wai	wei	wan	wen	wang	weng	yue	yuan	yun	yong
	⑱	⑲	⑳	㉑	㉒	㉓	㉔	㉕	㉖	㉗	㉘	㉙	㉚	㉛	㉜	㉝	㉞	㉟	㊱
	Group i Finals							Group u Finals								Group ü Finals			

APPENDIX

149

Answers to picture questions include the number of the picture and the correct pinyin. Pictures are counted from left to right.

UNIT 1

Part 1   1. (3) mǎ   2. (1) nán
          3. (2) fàn   4. (1) là

Part 2   1. o   2. i   3. a   4. i

Part 3   1. lǐ   2. fó   3. nà

UNIT 2

Part 1   1. (2) nǎi   2. (1) māo

Part 2   1. <u>l</u>ai   2. <u>n</u>ao   3. <u>m</u>ai   4. <u>l</u>ao

Part 3   1. láo   2. mài   3. máo

UNIT 3

Part 1   1. (2) lán   2. (3) láng

Part 2   1. na<u>n</u>   2. la<u>ng</u>   3. fa<u>ng</u>   4. la<u>n</u>

Part 3   1. lǎn   2. fàng   3. náng

REVIEW 1

Part 1   1. máo   2. nǎi
          3. mǐ   4. fáng
          5. nán

Part 2   1. Yes   2. No   3. No   4. Yes
          5. Yes   6. No

Part 3   1. nan   2. fang   3. la

Part 4

		l			
		à			
	l		n	ǎ	i
m	á	n	g		
	n				

UNIT 4

Part 1   1. (3) bái   2. (2) pán

Part 2   1. p   2. b   3. b   4. p

Part 3   1. pǎo   2. bào   3. pā

UNIT 5

Part 1   1. (3) dài   2. (1) tāng

Part 2   1. <u>d</u>āo   2. <u>t</u>án   3. <u>t</u>ào   4. <u>d</u>àng

Part 3   1. dà   2. tǎn   3. táng

UNIT 6

Part 1   1. (1) gāo   2. (3) kū
          3. (2) hǎi

Part 2   1. h   2. k   3. k   4. g

Part 3   1. kāi   2. hǎo   3. gāng

REVIEW 2

Part 1   1. dàn   2. gāo
       3. tāng   4. kàn
       5. bāozi

Part 2   1. Yes   2. No   3. No   4. No
       5. No   6. Yes

Part 3   1. tang   2. kao   3. dai

Part 4

		d		
		à		
p	à	n	g	
ă				
m	à	o		

UNIT 7

Part 1   1. (3) zǎo   2. (2) zhàng

Part 2   1. zài   2. zhào
       3. zhǎng   4. zá

Part 3   1. zì   2. zhān   3. zào

UNIT 8

Part 1   1. (3) cǎo   2. (1) chán

Part 2   1. cai   2. cháng
       3. chǎo   4. càn

Part 3   1. cì   2. cháng
       3. chá

UNIT 9

Part 1   1. (3) sǎn   2. (2) shàn
       3. (2) rǎn

Part 2   1. páshān   2. rìjì
       3. dǎsǎo

Part 3   1. shí   2. shāo   3. sān

REVIEW 3

Part 1   1. zhàng   2. zāng
       3. shàn   4. chá
       5. cài

Part 2

				s	ān
				ă	
				n	
c	h	á	n	g	
h					
s	ì				

Part 3   1. (5)(9)   2. (3)(8)
       3. (2)(6)   4. (4)(10)

Part 4   山 (shān, mountain)

UNIT 10

Part 1   1. (2) pò   2. (1) hǔ
       3. (2) gǒu

Part 2   1. pifu   2. dalou
       3. lao popo

Part 3   1. dù   2. lóu   3. bō

UNIT 11

Part 1   1. (2) hī   2. (3) bei

Part 2   1. keai   2. kuaile
       3. heiban

Part 3   1. fèi   2. zhē   3. lěi

UNIT 12

Part 1   1. (1) pèn   2. (2) fēng

Part 2   1. taideng   2. tengtong
          3. genhen

Part 3   1. děng   2. hěn
          3. gèng

REVIEW 4

Part 1   1. é   2. mén
          3. lěng   4. kǒu
          5. féi

Part 2

			2. 4. h	é
			ó	
	3. f		u	
1. g	ē	n		
	i			

Part 3   1. (3)(10)   2. (5)(7)
          3. (4)(8)   4. (2)(6)

Part 4   1. ei   2. en   3. ou   4. eng

UNIT 13

Part 1   1. shǒubiǎo   2. dìbǎn
          3. yàzhōu

Part 2   1. mǐ   2. yà   3. niǎo

Part 3   1. lí   2. biǎo   3. bǐ   4. yá
          5. niǎo

UNIT 14

Part 1   1. qiézi   2. diūdiào
          3. niúyóu

Part 2   1. tiě   2. yòu   3. liù

Part 3   1. niú   2. yóu   3. diē
          4. diū   5. yē

UNIT 15

Part 1   1. niúròumiàn   2. xiāngyān
          3. wǔ diǎn

Part 2   1. biàn   2. yǎng
          3. nián

Part 3   1. xiǎng   2. miàn
          3. yáng

UNIT 16

Part 1   1. dīngzi   2. yínháng
          3. píng'ān

Part 2   1. líng   2. qīng   3. pǐn

Part 3   1. bīng   2. tīng   3. lín

UNIT 17

Part 1   1. pínqióng   2. xiūxi
          3. xǐqìyángyáng

Part 2   1. xiǎng   2. qián   3. jiè

Part 3   1. xiào   2. qiú   3. qián
          4. jiǎo   5. xióng

REVIEW 5

Part 1 1. yè 2. yáng 3. yóu
4. lín 5. xiā

Part 2

		y		
	l			à
b	i	ǎ		o
	ǎ			
b	ī	n	g	

Part 3 1. (5)(7) 2. (1)(6)
3. (2)(8) 4. (3)(10)

Part 4 Yì wǎn niúròumiàn liù qiān liù.
(A bowl of beef noodle soup costs six thousand, six hundred dollars.)

UNIT 18

Part 1 1. luóbo 2. fùmǔ
3. huāpíng

Part 2 1. tù 2. kuā 3. duǒ

Part 3 1. huǒ 2. wā 3. huá
4. bù 5. zhū

UNIT 19

Part 1 1. shuāihuài 2. wāiwéi
3. kuàikuài shuì

Part 2 1. shuài 2. suí 3. guài

Part 3 1. kuài 2. guì 3. huài

UNIT 20

Part 1 1. chuángdān 2. suànzhàng
3. guānguāng

Part 2 1. chuāng 2. guàng
3. duǎn

Part 3 1. huáng 2. guāng
3. chuán

UNIT 21

Part 1 1. kōngqì 2. kūnchóng
3. nóngrén

Part 2 1. zhōng 2. sǔn
3. dòng

Part 3 1. dūn 2. gùn
3. hóng

153

REVIEW 6

Part 1   1. huáng   2. hǔ
         3. guō   4. huā
         5. chóng

Part 2

			4.	g
				u
				ā
	3.	k		n
1. h	u	á	n	g
	à			
2. x	i	à	o	

Part 3   1. (5)(10)   2. (4)(6)
         3. (2)(7)   4. (1)(9)

Part 4   Tā zuì xǐhuan huáng méigui.
         (She likes yellow roses best.)

UNIT 22

Part 1   1. jué   2. lǚ
         3. quē

Part 2   1. yuèqǔ   2. quántou
         3. yùyuē   4. nǚxù

Part 3   1. xuě   2. què
         3. yú

UNIT 23

Part 1   1. quān   2. xún
         3. juàn

Part 2   1. jūnzǐ   2. qúnzi
         3. lièquǎn   4. zuìxūnxūn

Part 3   1. juàn   2. yūn
         3. yuán

UNIT 24

Part 1   1. xiǎozhūr   2. shízir
         3. nǎr   4. yóupiàor

Part 2   1. nàr   2. huāqúnr
         3. lǎobànr   4. yǔdiǎnr

Part 3   1. huār   2. guǒzhīr
         3. dēngpàor

REVIEW 7

Part 1   1. xuě   2. yuán
         3. quǎn   4. yǔ
         5. yún

Part 2

		4.	x	
2.	q	u	ē	
		ǎ		
1. 3. y	u	à	n	
u				
è				

Part 3   1. x<u>ué</u>   2. nà<u>r</u>
         3. q<u>ún</u>   4. l<u>ǚ</u>
         5. w<u>ǎn</u>   6. gà<u>ir</u>

Part 4   1. qúnzi   2. júhuā
         3. yuèqǔ   4. xiàxuě
         5. xuǎn

154